# THE NEW MIDDLE EAST
## WHAT EVERYONE NEEDS TO KNOW®

# THE NEW MIDDLE EAST

## WHAT EVERYONE NEEDS TO KNOW®

*Second Edition*

## JAMES L. GELVIN

OXFORD
UNIVERSITY PRESS

# OXFORD
UNIVERSITY PRESS

Oxford University Press is a department of the University of Oxford. It furthers the University's objective of excellence in research, scholarship, and education by publishing worldwide. Oxford is a registered trade mark of Oxford University Press in the UK and certain other countries.

"What Everyone Needs to Know" is a registered trademark of Oxford University Press.

Published in the United States of America by Oxford University Press 198 Madison Avenue, New York, NY 10016, United States of America.

Library of Congress Cataloging-in-Publication Data
Names: Gelvin, James L., 1951- author.
Title: The new Middle East : what everyone needs to know / James L. Gelvin.
Description: Second edition. | New York, NY : Oxford University Press, [2023] |
Series: What everyone needs to know |
Includes bibliographical references and index.
Identifiers: LCCN 2023032477 (print) | LCCN 2023032478 (ebook) |
ISBN 9780197622094 (pb) | ISBN 9780197622087 (hb) | ISBN 9780197622117 (e)
Subjects: LCSH: Middle East—Politics and government—21st century. |
Middle East—History. | Arab Spring, 2010- | IS (Organization)—History. |
Middle East—Foreign relations—21st century. | Human security—Middle East.
Classification: LCC DS63.123 .G45 2023 (print) | LCC DS63.123 (ebook) |
DDC 320.9/56—dc23/eng/20230713
LC record available at https://lccn.loc.gov/2023032477
LC ebook record available at https://lccn.loc.gov/2023032478

DOI: 10.1093/wentk/9780197622087.001.0001

Paperback printed by Sheridan Books, Inc., United States of America
Hardback printed by Bridgeport National Bindery, Inc., United States of America

# CONTENTS

## 3. Things Fall Apart                                                 52

# PREFACE

I am a historian by training and trade. Although I began my career as a specialist in early-twentieth-century Syria, the on-rush of events in the Middle East and the insatiable appetite of the general public for information that might help it better understand the region encouraged me to shift my focus to what is called "contemporary history"—a phrase that seems more a contradiction in terms than an established subfield of history. Hence my book, *The Arab Uprisings: What Everyone Needs to Know*, also published by Oxford University Press.

One of the greatest practitioners of my trade, Fernand Braudel, once wrote that anyone who tries to understand current affairs by focusing only on today and the immediate past "will continually have his eye caught by anything that moves quickly or glitters." However (he continued), a knowledge of history enables us "to know whether what one is witnessing is the rise of a new movement, the tail end of an old one, an echo from the very distant past, or a monotonously recurring phenomenon."[1] History matters: it is embedded in the present (or, as novelist William Faulkner put it, "The past is never dead. It's not even past."[2]). And so I wrote this book to apply what I have learned over the years to ongoing events.

I am grateful for the encouragement and hard work of my editor at Oxford University Press, Nancy Toff, and her assistants, Elda Granata and Elizabeth Vaziri (for the first edition) and Chelsea Hogue (for the second). I am also grateful to those who reviewed the manuscript for the first edition of this book, whose criticisms and suggestions made it all the better. Finally, I am grateful to my students at UCLA who, on multiple occasions, patiently sat through seminars and lectures concerning many of the issues raised in this book while I honed my arguments and put them in a comprehensible form.

Earlier renditions of parts of this book first appeared on the online websites History News Network and The Conversation. I have also drawn from my print publications, including *The Arab Uprisings: What Everyone Needs to Know*, 2nd ed. (New York: Oxford University Press, 2015); The Modern Middle East: A History, 4th ed. (New York: Oxford University Press, 2015); and "The Arab World at the Intersection of the Transnational and National," in David W. Lesch and Mark Haas (eds.), The Arab Spring: Hope and Reality of the Uprisings, 2nd ed. (Boulder, CO: Westview Press, 2012).

# THE NEW MIDDLE EAST

## WHAT EVERYONE NEEDS TO KNOW®

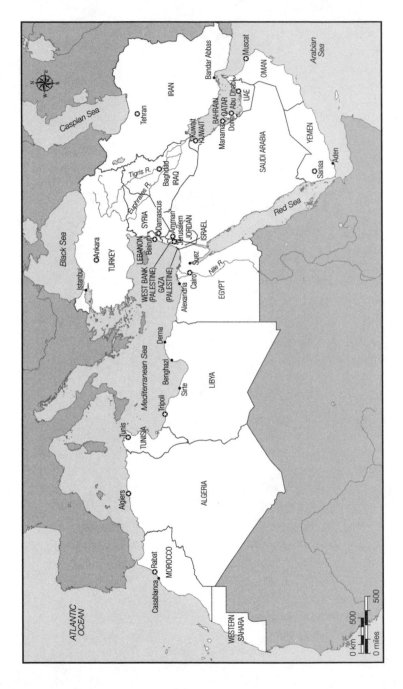

**Map 1** The Middle East

# 1

# BEFORE THE DELUGE

## THE MIDDLE EAST, 1945–2011

### What is the Middle East?

"Middle East" is one of several terms that refer to the territory of southwest Asia and North Africa. Other terms for the same region include Greater Middle East, Near East, and Middle East and North Africa (MENA).

Although now commonplace, the term "Middle East" is of recent vintage. It was coined in the first years of the twentieth century. At the time, it referred only to the area surrounding the Persian Gulf. In 1920, the British Royal Geographic Society recommended its use to refer to the area stretching from the Turkish Straits in the west to the frontier of India in the east. Nevertheless, it did not displace "Near East" in British and US policy circles until World War II. But even after the term passed into general usage, the boundaries of the region remained imprecise and a bit arbitrary. Is Sudan, an Arab state bordering Egypt in the south, part of the Middle East? What about Armenia?

In this book, "Middle East" refers to the territory that stretches from Morocco in the west to Iran in the east. It includes Morocco, Algeria, Tunisia, Libya, and Egypt (but not Sudan—boundaries have to be drawn somewhere) in North Africa, and Syria, Lebanon, Israel, Palestine, Jordan, Iraq, Iran, Kuwait, Saudi Arabia, Bahrain, Qatar, the United Arab Emirates (UAE), Oman, and Yemen (but not Armenia—again, for the same reason) in southwest Asia. It also includes Turkey, which straddles Europe and southwest Asia.

## Who lives in the Middle East?

According to the World Bank, as of 2020 there were approximately 538 million people living in the Middle East.[1] This statistic must, however, be treated with some skepticism. For example, Lebanon has not conducted a census since 1932. Doing so might invalidate the agreed-upon formula for proportional representation among the various religious groups living there. Because of conscription in Egypt, parents do not always register the births of their sons. And although the World Bank puts the population of Qatar at close to 2.9 million, that statistic fails to take into account that more than 88 percent of the people living in Qatar are temporary guest workers. There are about 336,000 Qatari citizens.

Whatever the number of inhabitants of the region, however, those who live there represent a broad array of ethnic, linguistic, and religious groups. The three largest ethnic groups are Arabs, Turks, and Iranians. Arabs make up the overwhelming majority. Estimates of the number of Arabs in the Middle East run between 300 million and 345 million, although these numbers, like most official statistics, must be taken with more than a grain of salt. Most Arabs, Turks, and Iranians live in the Arab world, Turkey, and Iran, respectively. But Arabs, Turks, and Iranians live outside those areas as well. Arab populations live in both Turkey and Iran, ethnically Turkish tribes live in Iran, and Iranian refugees live in both Iraq and Turkey.

Other ethnic groups in the region include Kurds and Berbers. Kurds live mainly in Turkey, Iraq, Syria, and Iran. Clocking in at upward of thirty-five million, they represent the world's largest stateless nation. Most Berbers live in North Africa. Because the term "Berber" can refer both to those who descend from the inhabitants of the region who lived there before the Arab conquest in the eighth century as well as to those whose native language is Tamazight (Berber), estimates of the number of Berbers vary widely.

The Middle East is also linguistically diverse. The native language of most Arabs and Turks is, of course, Arabic and Turkish, but Farsi (also known as Persian) is the native language of only about half the population of Iran. Other ethnic groups in the region have their own native languages, such as Kurdish, Tamazight, and Armenian. And in Israel, Hebrew is the official language (as was Arabic until 2018).

A majority of the inhabitants of the Middle East are Muslim. There are two main branches of Islam—Sunni Islam and Shiʻi Islam. The split in the Islamic community took place after the death of Muhammad, when his followers disagreed about who should lead the community. Over time, each branch developed different rituals, traditions, and beliefs. Understanding that there is a divide between Sunnis and Shiʻis is important for understanding some of the political rivalries in the region. It is important to note, however, that the rivalries that pit members of the two communities against each other concern political issues, such as which group should govern. They rarely concern religious issues per se. Where sects contend against each other, religion merely acts as an identifier of the political community to which one belongs. Therefore, understanding how each community's rituals, traditions, and beliefs differ from the other's is not at all important for understanding the New Middle East.

Most Arabs and Turks are Sunnis, although Shiʻis make up a significant minority in Lebanon, Yemen, Kuwait, and Saudi Arabia. They make up a majority in two other Arab countries, Bahrain and Iraq. Most Iranians are Shiʻis, and Iran is the world's largest Shiʻi country.

There are other religious groups in the region as well. Christians of various stripes—Orthodox, Catholics, Maronites (mainly in Lebanon), Copts (mainly in Egypt)—live throughout the Middle East. After the establishment of the State of Israel, most of the members of the Arab world's once flourishing

Jewish communities quit their homelands voluntarily or because they were coerced to do so by their governments. The largest number decamped to Israel. A similar exodus of Iranian Jews took place after the establishment of the Islamic Republic in 1979. Then there are a myriad of other religious groups as well, including Zaydis in Yemen, Alawites in Syria and Turkey, Alevis in Turkey, Yazidis in Iraq and Syria, Ibadis in Oman and North Africa, and Druze in Israel, Syria, Lebanon, and Jordan. Again, the fact that these groups are present in the region is, at times, an important element in our story.

### What is the Middle East state system?

The year 2016 marked the hundredth anniversary of the Sykes-Picot Agreement, and there were countless op-eds and commentaries commemorating (bemoaning?) it. This agreement was a plan hatched during World War I by two officials, Sir Mark Sykes of the British War Office and François Georges-Picot, the French consul in Beirut, to divide up the Asiatic provinces of the Ottoman Empire in the aftermath of the war. The Ottoman Empire, which ruled much of the Asiatic Arab world as well as Anatolia (the site of present-day Turkey) and Egypt, had entered the war on the side of the Central Powers, which Britain, France, and their allies were fighting.

Ever since, Sykes-Picot has come to symbolize the artificial nature of state boundaries in the Middle East. According to most of the op-eds and commentaries written on the occasion of the anniversary, we have instability in the region today because these boundaries were drawn by far-off diplomats who had no regard for the wishes of the populations living there.

Or at least that is the story. The reality is quite different. The boundaries Mark Sykes and François Georges-Picot drew up would have been no more or less artificial than any other boundaries that separate states—had they actually gone into effect. They did not. The British, whose military actually occupied the territory covered by the agreement, were dissatisfied with the boundaries, and the French were powerless to complain. In other words, by the end of World War I the agreement was already a dead letter.

How, then, did states in the territory covered by the agreement (which, by the way, included only a tiny fraction of the territory of the Middle East) get their boundaries? In the Asiatic Arab territories, a number of states had their boundaries set through the mandates system, which the League of Nations, the precursor to the United Nations, instituted there. The system allotted Britain and France temporary control over territory in the region. The two powers took it upon themselves to combine or divide territories into proto-states in accordance with their imperial interests. Thus, Britain created Iraq and Trans-Jordan (later the Hashemite Kingdom of Jordan, or simply Jordan) after the war. Israel and Palestine came even later. France did the same for Lebanon and Syria.

Those states, like most others in the Middle East, gained their independence during two waves. The first wave took place during the period between World War I and World War II. Iraq, Saudi Arabia, and Turkey achieved independence then, and Egypt became somewhat independent (Iran and Oman—the latter known then as Muscat and Oman—were already independent states). The British granted independence to its mandate, Iraq, mainly because remaining there would have been a drain on the imperial treasury. They almost did the same for Egypt, which they had been occupying since 1882. After a widespread rebellion convinced them that Egypt would be ungovernable unless changes were made, they granted Egypt "conditional independence" in 1922. It took Egyptians almost thirty-five years to eliminate the British role there entirely and change conditional independence into full independence.

Saudi Arabia and Turkey achieved independence on the battlefield. In the former case, Abdulaziz ibn Saud, a warlord from north/central Arabia, led an army composed of warriors from a mix of tribes that conquered much of the Arabian Peninsula. When the dust had settled, he established a dynasty that has ruled Saudi Arabia to this day. In Anatolia, Turkish nationalists fought a grueling four-year war that drove out foreigners who had been occupying the peninsula since the end of World War I. The result was the contemporary Republic of Turkey.

The second wave of state construction took place during the Period of Decolonization, which began after World War II and lasted through the first half of the 1970s. The Period of Decolonization marked the end of formal British, French, and Portuguese colonial empires. During this period, Morocco, Algeria, Tunisia, Lebanon, and Syria gained their independence from France (Spain also abandoned most of the territory it controlled in Morocco). Much of the Gulf (the UAE, Qatar, Bahrain, and Kuwait), along with Israel and Jordan, gained theirs from Britain.

None of these places had been colonies, per se. There had been only one real colony in the Middle East—the British colony of Aden. After independence, Aden became, first, part of South Yemen, then part of Yemen (established in 1990 when North Yemen merged with South Yemen). Instead of colonies, the British and French empires in the Middle East consisted mainly of mandates and protectorates (proto-states in which local rulers set domestic policy and kept order while Britain and France handled their dealings with the rest of the world). There was also the occasional occupation (Egypt) or the wholesale integration of territory into the mother country (as in the case of Algeria, which the French considered as much a part of France as Paris until its independence in 1962). Libya, which the Italians had integrated into Italy in like fashion, also became an independent state during this period. Captured by the Allies from the Italians during World War II, Libya became a ward of the United Nations, which granted it independence three years after the organization's founding.

Some states in the region—Turkey, Israel, Algeria—won their independence through armed struggle. Others—most of the mandates, for example—won it through negotiation. And some—Saudi Arabia, Yemen—went through painful periods before the state-building process was over. Then there is the unique case of Palestine. Palestinians engaged in armed struggle with Israel for forty-five years before joining their opponent in direct negotiations. Short bursts of negotiation, separated by periods of breakdown and conflict, continued thereafter. The United Nations voted to recognize Palestine as a nonvoting observer state in 2012.

In spite of its motley origins and the lamentations of those who hold on to the myth of Sykes-Picot, the Middle East state system has been remarkably stable ever since the end of the Period of Decolonization. There have been exceptions, of course, including the shifting borders of Israel and the unification of North and South Yemen in 1990. Nevertheless, the state system in the Middle East has been one of the most stable state systems in the world. It certainly has been more stable than the state system in Europe.

There are two reasons for this stability. First, the passage of time. Although most member states of the state system in the region received their complete independence after World War II, the process of formulating distinct national identities began while those states were under foreign rule. Ever since, states engaged their citizens in common practices and worked to develop their own internal markets and divisions of labor. These are necessary (but obviously not sufficient) preconditions for the formation of distinct national identities. The states in the region also jealously guarded their borders, rewrote their histories, and, indeed, produced enough of their own histories to differentiate their national experience from that of their neighbors. As a result, with the exception of Yemen, no attempt to adjust state borders by negotiation—including the short-lived union between Egypt and Syria (the United Arab Republic, 1958–1961)—bore fruit during the postcolonial era.

The second reason the state system has been relatively stable has been support for that system provided by great powers—first Britain, then the United States—and by regional actors anxious to maintain the status quo. Great power intervention has occurred whenever some strongman or national liberation movement has risen to the surface and threatened to upset the balance of power or great power interests. Britain twice intervened in Oman (1959, 1975) to crush rebellions that threatened to divide the country. The British again intervened in the Gulf in 1961 to protect newly independent Kuwait from its northern neighbor, which claimed it as Iraq's nineteenth province. Iraq's Saddam Hussein reasserted that claim in 1990. Once again, foreign intervention forced an Iraqi retreat.

### Do the states in the Middle East have anything in common?

At first glance, the states in the Middle East seem as varied as the people who inhabit the region. The Middle East includes twelve republics and eight monarchies. Egypt has a population of over 100 million (the populations of Turkey and Iran are both a little over eighty million), while the populations of Bahrain and Qatar are 1.7 million and 2.2 million, respectively—if you include guest workers. Algeria, geographically the largest state in the region, spans close to one million square miles. Bahrain, the smallest, includes fewer than three hundred. Then there are the differences in wealth. At its height in 2011, the average annual income of each citizen of Qatar, the richest country in the Middle East, was $148,000. That same year it was $2,600 in Yemen, the poorest. In 2020, after COVID-19 and years of civil strife, that number fell to $2,213.

Nevertheless, beneath the apparent variations among the countries of the region, there are some striking similarities. From the Period of Decolonization through the last decades of the twentieth century, governments throughout the region (Lebanon excepted) played a major role in the economy. They did so to force-march economic development, expand employment opportunities, reward favored groups in the population, and gain control over strategic industries. Governments also provided a wide array of social benefits for their populations, including employment guarantees, health care, and education. In addition, governments subsidized consumer goods.

There were several reasons why governments in the region—and, indeed, throughout the developing world—adopted these policies. The United States encouraged them to do so, believing that a combination of economic development and welfare would create stable, pro-Western states. So did international financial institutions, such as the World Bank and the International Monetary Fund (IMF), and a legion of development experts who passed on cookie-cutter policies wherever they went. These policies fit the economic paradigm popular at the time. That paradigm gave pride of place to full employment and rising standards of living as the two indicators of economic success. Governments, it was believed, could guide resources to ensure that both goals were reached more effectively in environments in which markets were not well developed.

The third factor leading to the adoption of these economic policies was the logic of decolonization. Before independence, imperial powers set economic policy, mainly for their own benefit. With independence, governments asserted their economic rights to make up for lost time. They also attempted to win domestic support through the redistribution of national wealth.

To pay the cost of development and their welfare policies, almost all states in the region depended on a type of revenue known as "rent." Rent is revenue that states derive from sources other than taxation. The Middle East as a whole is the most rent-dependent region in the world.

The most obvious source of rent in the region is oil. As of 2018, oil exports accounted for 87 percent of Saudi Arabia's revenue and 90 percent of Kuwait's and Iraq's (other major oil producers, such as Qatar and the UAE, have had more success diversifying their economies). But there have been other sources of rent as well. Egypt derives much of its revenue from foreign aid, Suez Canal tolls, and hydrocarbon (oil and natural gas) exports. Syria has received foreign aid both from countries that have wanted to keep it out of mischief and from countries that have wanted to encourage that mischief. And over the course of its lifetime, Israel's rent income has come in the form of American aid (around $3 billion each year in the form of direct military aid since Israel signed a peace treaty with Egypt in 1979), reparations from Germany for the Holocaust, and contributions and loans from Jews living abroad.

In the Arab world, dependence on rent has shaped the relationship between states and their citizens. Access to rent not only means that the state does not have to solicit revenue from its citizens, it also ensures that the state will be the dominant economic actor. This has enabled the state to attach itself to its population through ties of patronage. It also makes it possible for states to temper or buy off dissent—although, as governments throughout the Arab world have increasingly discovered since the 1980s, loyalty has to be earned as well as bought. Overall, states' access to rent in the Arab world reinforces a relationship between the state and its citizens—what political scientists call the "ruling bargain"—that can be summed up in the phrase "benefits for compliance": Sit down, shut up, and we'll take care of you.

Just as the norms of the global economic and political systems shaped states in the Middle East from the Period of Decolonization through the late 1970s, so, too, did a different set of norms that spread worldwide thereafter. If the first period was one in which the state was to play an active role in guiding development and providing welfare, the second was one in which the state was to back off and play a minimal role. As the theory went, free trade and a market-driven approach to economics would enable the sorts of economic gains that had proved so elusive under the old system. This doctrine came to be known as neo-liberalism.

Neo-liberalism began as a response to the international economic crisis of the 1970s. American policy makers saw it as a panacea for a host of ills, including the threat to America's dominant position in the world economy and the inability of the overextended governments in the developing world to meet their international economic obligations. The American government therefore pushed rigorously for neo-liberalism wherever diplomats gathered to decide global economic policy. They were assisted in their efforts by the IMF, an organization which the United States dominated and whose job it was to assist countries whose economies had tanked. If those countries needed loans, or if they merely wanted to be deemed creditworthy, the IMF insisted they undertake structural "reforms" to set them on the right path. Only then did the IMF render the necessary assistance.

Neo-liberalism reshaped states, their institutions, and their relationship to their populations. With governments no longer responsible for guaranteeing full employment and social welfare, neo-liberal experts from the IMF and their partners inside governments advised those governments to sell off state-owned enterprises to private investors, reduce tariff barriers and currency controls to promote trade, balance their budgets, deregulate business, and the like. The result was rarely pretty. Popular resistance, corruption, and entrenched interests prevented the realization of the neo-liberal dream in most of the region (if, indeed, it is realizable). Thus, the overall effect of neo-liberal policies in most states was to overlay a jury-rigged market economy on top of an inefficient command economy. At the same time, neo-liberalism shredded the "benefits for compliance" ruling bargain that connected populations with their governments.

### What was political life like in the Middle East up through 2010?

Every year, the Economist Intelligence Unit publishes a "Democracy Index."[2] The index ranks countries of the world according to such criteria as electoral process and pluralism, civil liberties, the functioning of government, political participation, and political culture. It then places each country in one of five categories that range from "full democracies" to "authoritarian regimes." How did the Middle East fare in 2010, the year in which the first of the Arab uprisings broke out?

Not well. In 2010 not one state in the Middle East made it into the category of "full democracy." Only one state—Israel—made it into the category of "flawed democracy," coming in at a ranking of #37 among all the countries of the world. In flawed democracies there are free and fair elections and respect for basic civil liberties. However, there are significant weaknesses in other democratic practices, including problems in governance. The next-highest-ranked state in the region was Lebanon (#86), followed by Turkey (#89), Palestine (#93), and Iraq (#111). *The Economist* called these states "hybrid democracies." Elections in all four had substantial irregularities, corruption was widespread, and nongovernmental institutions were weak. (A decade later, Lebanon's ranking had dropped to #108, Turkey's to #104, Palestine's to #113, and Iraq's to #118.)

All fifteen of the remaining countries in the Middle East fit into the category "authoritarian regimes." The lowest-ranked state was Saudi Arabia, which came in at #160 on a scale in which the lowest ranking overall was #167. On the whole, the Middle East had the lowest composite score of any region in the world, with the exception of sub-Saharan Africa.

From the different rankings on *The Economist* list, it is evident that the level of autocracy was not uniform across the region. Autocratic regimes came in various shapes and sizes. Although Kuwait (#114) and Jordan (#117), for example, are monarchies like Saudi Arabia, both have parliaments which can, at times, be defiant. Saudi Arabia does not. Nevertheless, in all three, kings maintain ultimate control: kings can dismiss prime ministers and appoint cabinets. Furthermore, in Kuwait and Jordan electoral districts are heavily gerrymandered.

Before its uprising, Egypt had a form of government that one political scientist called "semi-authoritarian."[3] In other words, the government allowed the opposition (the main component of which during the pre-uprising period was the Egyptian

Muslim Brotherhood) some ability to organize and compete in elections, but no opportunity to win them. A United Nations report called Egypt, like most other Arab states, a "black hole state," meaning that the executive branch—that is, the office of president or king—was so powerful that it "converts the surrounding environment into a setting in which nothing moves and from which nothing escapes."[4]

Libya under its "brotherly leader" Muammar Qaddafi (who ruled from 1969 to 2011), on the other hand, claimed to have no government at all. Instead, it was a *jamahirriya*, a word made up by Qaddafi to mean "rule by the masses." Qaddafi maintained that Libya was a direct democracy in which everyone participated in governance without the mediation of representatives. Since such a system could not possibly work, Libya had, in fact, two governments: a "people's government" on paper and a real government, made up of Qaddafi, his kin, and those he favored, which actually ran the country. Libya narrowly beat out Saudi Arabia on *The Economist* index, tying Iran—an Islamic republic in which clerics, in alliance with the military, hold ultimate power—at #158.

Hybrid democracies differ in form as well as in ranking. For example, the Lebanese system might be termed a "sectarian oligarchy." Voters can choose their leaders from a list of the same old political bosses whose posts are determined by the religious sect to which they belong. In Turkey, hybrid democracy works until it doesn't. The culprit there has usually been the army, which assumed power in 1960, 1971, and 1980; forced the resignation of a prime minister in 1997; and tried (and failed) to take power again in 2016. Each time it assumed power, the army relinquished it only after "cleansing" the political system. It did this by disbanding parties and jailing (and frequently torturing) those it deemed enemies of the state. (Turkey is once again on an authoritarian path, but this time the guilty party—the president—dresses in civilian clothes.) On the other hand, weak institutions and corrupt and incompetent governance threaten the very integrity of both Iraq and Palestine (which has had two competing governments since 2007).

## How did state formation in the region breed autocracies in the Middle East?

Autocratic structures were inscribed into the DNA of most states in the Middle East early on. The independent states that emerged in the region might be divided into three categories. First, there are those that emerged in the interwar period— Turkey, Iran, and Saudi Arabia. In all three, militaries played a key role in establishing the states, and military leaders became their initial rulers. Autocrats in Iran and Saudi Arabia both benefited from foreign (British) support and, in the case of the latter, the British offered protection to the future ruler before the state was founded. And it didn't hurt that autocratic models of state building and governance were readily available in a period during which Lenin, Hitler, and Mussolini took and held power.

The second category of state includes those that retained the structures the colonial powers had put in place or had sheltered after independence. Those powers had been interested in stability, not democracy. The states in this category include not only most of the remaining monarchies (Morocco, Jordan, Bahrain, Qatar, Kuwait, and the UAE), but Lebanon as well (Oman's relationship with Britain was more informal but significant nonetheless). The British and French viewed monarchs as reliable collaborators so long as they governed with a firm hand. As in Lebanon, the path to independence taken by monarchies was mainly peaceful (in the Gulf it was the British, not the various monarchs, who insisted that the statelets cut the cord). As a result, their transition from the colonial to the postcolonial era was marked more by continuity than rupture.

The final category of state consists of the postcolonial republics that took shape with the overthrow of the colonial order after independence: Tunisia (where a civilian wrested control of the government, abolishing the monarchy), Algeria, Libya, Egypt, Syria, Iraq, and Yemen. Again, timing was everything: With the exception of Yemen—created through a shotgun wedding between two formerly independent Yemens in 1990—all emerged at the height of decolonization, when anti-imperialist revolutions and coups d'état undertaken by colonels hell-bent on destroying the remnants of the old order were the tactic du jour. Revolutionaries and coup plotters had little patience with democratic niceties. Their stated goals were typically to end the imperialist presence in their countries, to end feudalism (meaning, economic backwardness), and to end "corruption" (their term for the old boys' club of the former regime, which they sought to break up).

The Islamic Republic of Iran might also be placed in this category. Like Algeria, the Islamic republic was born of a mass uprising. And like all the others in this category, its leaders sought to root out most vestiges of the old regime.

### How did great power meddling in the region foster autocracies in the Middle East?

In November 2003, President George W. Bush spoke before the National Endowment for Democracy and announced his "Freedom Agenda." "Sixty years of Western nations excusing and accommodating the lack of freedom in the Middle East did nothing to make us safe—because in the long run, stability cannot be purchased at the expense of liberty," he declared. "As long as the Middle East remains a place where freedom does not flourish, it will remain a place of stagnation, resentment, and violence ready for export."[5] He then announced what he called a "forward" strategy to advance freedom in the region.

Two years after he gave that speech, his secretary of state, Condoleezza Rice, paid a visit to Egypt to meet with Egyptian president Hosni Mubarak. She took the occasion to address students at the American University in Cairo. In her speech she reiterated Bush's remarks. "For sixty years, my country, the United States, pursued stability at the expense of democracy in this region here in the Middle East—and we achieved neither. Now, we are taking a different course. We are supporting the democratic aspirations of all people."[6]

A year and a half later, however, Rice changed her tune. Instead of pressuring Mubarak about human rights and democracy during a return visit to Cairo, she instead appealed for his help in restarting stalled negotiations between Israelis and Palestinians. The Bush administration's much vaunted, but fleeting, concern for spreading American values had gone the way of other initiatives to put values ahead of immediate strategic need. American policy reverted to its default position, which one political scientist has termed "democracy prevention."[7] Why haven't American actions matched American rhetoric?

Over the course of the twentieth century, great powers— meaning first Great Britain, then the United States—established states, intervened directly into their internal affairs, or both. They also protected those states from internal and external threats. Great powers have used their leverage in both the political and economic spheres to dictate policy to governments and have granted them financial assistance. Underwriting democracy was not a high priority for those powers.

Great Britain was the predominant power in the region past the end of World War II. That status was not to last. In the aftermath of the war, the United States, which had never before had an equivalent stake in the region, took Britain's place as the predominant power. In part this had to do with British economic weakness and American economic strength. The United States, fearing the spread of communism in the Gulf, even offered to pay the insolvent British to remain there. In part this had to do with the ability of the United States to insinuate itself into the conflict between Israel and the states that surrounded it as an indispensable broker during the 1970s. And in part this had to do with the role the United States played as leader of the "free world" during the Cold War.

American engagement with the region coincided with the onset of the Cold War, which defined US goals there. Paramount among those goals was to contain the Soviet Union and prevent the spread of its influence to the strategically located, oil-rich region. To this end, autocratic regimes proved useful to the United States. For example, American policy makers believed that only strong, autocratic regimes could bring about the rapid economic development necessary to prevent their populations from "going communist." Only strong, autocratic regimes such as that in Egypt, they believed, could sign peace treaties with Israel in the face of popular opposition to those treaties. And, they believed, only strong, autocratic regimes that maintained a regional balance of power could ensure the uninterrupted supply of oil to the United States and its allies.

The United States directly and indirectly supported military officers who seized power in states throughout the region from the late 1940s through the 1960s. For example, the United States backed (some say sponsored) the first post-independence coup d'état in Syria—the first coup in the Arab world following World War II. The coup overthrew a democratically elected government. And, of course, the United States directly and indirectly supported a host of autocratic kings and emirs. This began even before the end of World War II, when Saudi Arabia became the only neutral state to receive American Lend-Lease assistance.

When the Cold War ended, the United States maintained its support for autocratic regimes, in part out of a sense of obligation and repayment for loyalty, in part because policymakers preferred stability in international relations to anything that might disrupt that stability, in part out of habit. Thus, for example, the United States headed the coalition that threw Iraq out of Kuwait in 1991. By doing so, it maintained the Middle East state system and balance of power as it had been before the invasion. It also assured the uninterrupted flow of oil. The United States then turned its back on Kuwaiti pro-democracy groups agitating for truly representative institutions in the kingdom.

After 9/11, the United States declared the Global War on Terrorism. This proved a boon to friend and foe alike. Autocrats such as Hosni Mubarak of Egypt, Ali Abdullah Saleh of Yemen, and even Muammar Qaddafi of Libya and Bashar al-Assad of Syria managed to put themselves on the side of angels. Mubarak and Assad accepted and interrogated suspected terrorists using torture, Saleh allowed the United States to fight its war on terror on his country's soil, and Qaddafi renounced his weapons of mass destruction. Interestingly, the Global War of Terrorism, which George W. Bush announced even before the Freedom Agenda, was one of the reasons the former president abandoned America's fleeting interest in promoting democracy.

### How has the exploitation of oil affected the Middle East?

Ever since the British Royal Navy switched from coal to oil to fuel its ships in the early twentieth century, Middle Eastern oil has loomed large in the strategic calculus of great powers. Hence, the United States and Britain organized a coup d'état that overthrew the democratically elected prime minister of Iran in 1953. His crime? He nationalized the British-owned oil company that operated in his country. Hence, the Fifth Fleet patrols the waters of the Persian Gulf. And hence, ongoing American support for some of the most hideous regimes on the planet that keep the oil flowing. Myanmar got sanctions; Saudi Arabia got F-15 Eagles.

Although oil began to flow from the Arabian Peninsula in 1938, Middle Easterners themselves did not begin to feel the revolutionary effects of oil production until the 1970s. That was when the oil-producing states in the region and elsewhere launched successful campaigns to wrest control of the pricing, production quotas, and ownership of their oil from the foreign-owned oil companies that had dominated the business until then. As a result of these campaigns, an unprecedented amount of wealth flowed into the Middle East.

What became known as the "oil price revolution"—the 380 percent increase in the price of oil during four months in 1973–1974—transformed the Arabian Peninsula from a cultural and political backwater into a regional powerhouse. Within ten years, oil exporters—the wealthiest of which were concentrated in the region at the time—had accumulated $1.7 trillion. The Gulf exporters in particular used this money to win friends and influence people. From 1973 to 1978, for example, Egypt alone received $17 billion from Arab oil producers in the form of grants and loans. Between 1973 and 1983, assistance from abroad paid for *all* of North Yemen's government spending. With small populations and weak militaries, Gulf states were thus able to punch above their diplomatic weight. It is no coincidence that the peace accord that ended the fifteen-year Lebanese civil war in 1989 is called the Taif Agreement, after the city in Saudi Arabia where it was negotiated.

Oil producers maintained leverage over their neighbors through labor policies as well. Because of their small size, the newly enriched oil producers had to rely on guest workers to keep their recharged economies humming and to build infrastructure. Initially, those guest workers came from the Arab world. In 1968, for example, no more than ten thousand Egyptians worked abroad. Within ten years, that number had increased to over half a million. A decade later, another million Egyptian workers found employment in Iraq. Sending their excess labor abroad benefited the states in the region that were not blessed with oil. It enabled them to sidestep the disquieting consequences of high unemployment. In addition, the money those workers sent home to their families reduced the burden of providing welfare and services for cash-strapped governments. Importing labor provided oil-rich states with an opportunity to coerce or punish their neighbors. Thus, when Egypt joined the Gulf War coalition, Iraq expelled its resident Egyptians.

Although Arabs initially made up a vast majority of guest workers in the Gulf, the Gulf states feared those workers might bring with them politically and socially subversive ideas which, as Arabic speakers, they might spread to native populations. As a result, Gulf states increasingly looked to their own populations for labor—a policy called "job nationalization." They also looked to South Asia. In 1975, 90 percent of the foreign workers in the Gulf came from Arab countries; twenty years later, that number had dropped to 38 percent. This, of course, closed the social safety valve upon which non–oil producers had come to rely.

The oil price revolution had two other effects on the region. First, it made the entire region—not just the oil producers—overly dependent on global markets. When the price of oil goes down, so do national incomes. And even though most oil-rich states have placed a sizable chunk of their earnings in sovereign wealth funds (state-owned investment funds) just in case, cashing in even a modest amount of those funds would depress the markets in which they are invested, thus lowering their value.

In addition, direct and indirect rent income from oil has contributed to the number and durability of autocracies in the region. Throughout the Arab world, states do not have to go to their populations, hat in hand, soliciting money. And oil revenue has provided states the wherewithal to subsidize welfare and services for their citizens, manipulate public attitudes and behaviors, and fight external aggression and domestic insurrection. As events since 2010 demonstrate, the use of money derived from oil for these purposes has not been foolproof. But it is not to be discounted, either.

## What is the "New Middle East"?

If credit is to be given to anyone for coining the phrase "New Middle East," that credit should go to Condoleezza Rice. In 2006, Israel invaded Lebanon. The invasion came in response to a cross-border raid and rocket attacks launched at Israel from Lebanon by Hizbullah, a Lebanese group that is a combination of militia, political party, and service provider. Nevertheless, the damage inflicted by the Israeli army on Lebanon was appalling, even by Middle East standards: Between 800 and 1,200 Lebanese died, many of them civilians (UNICEF estimated that upward of one third of the victims were children under the age of thirteen). Estimates of the damage to Lebanese infrastructure hovered around $2.5 billion.

In the midst of the carnage, Rice held a press conference at which she declared that what the world was witnessing in Lebanon was the "birth pangs of a new Middle East."[8] What Rice meant was that slapping down groups like Hizbullah would clear the way for the emergence of a more peaceful and democratic region. While Hizbullah was hardly slapped down, she was, in a way, correct: The war did herald the emergence of a new Middle East—one that was significantly more violent and unpredictable than its predecessor.

About a year and a half after Rice's comment, an American diplomat and policy analyst, Richard N. Haass, wrote an article for the journal *Foreign Affairs*, titled "The New Middle East."[9] According to Haass, the era of the "old" Middle East, defined in large measure by *pax Americana* ("American peace"), had drawn to a close. It had ended as a result of the American invasion of Iraq, the collapse of the Israeli-Palestinian peace process, the failure of Arab regimes to deal with radical Islam, and globalization. He then outlined twelve distinctive features of the era that was just beginning. While recounting them all is unnecessary here, suffice it to say that given the unforeseeable events of the 2010s, most of Haass's predictions were remarkably prescient.

In the chapters that follow, this book explores the contours of the New Middle East. Although it might be argued that the impact of twenty-first-century events on the region pales in comparison to the impact of, for example, nineteenth-century imperialism or World War I, it cannot be denied that the impact is, nevertheless, significant. Indeed, it is entirely possible that those events will leave a permanent mark on the politics, economics, society, and even demography of the region.

Three events gave rise to the New Middle East. The first was the collapse of the Soviet Union in 1991. That collapse marked the demise of the overarching American strategy in the region, along with the unity of purpose that joined the United States with its partners there. The American invasion of Iraq was, in large measure, a symptom of a superpower's floundering to find a new strategy, if not purpose, in the region. It would not have occurred during the Cold War lest the United States take its eyes off the prize of containing the Soviet Union.

The second and third events not only set the stage for the New Middle East, they played a key role in shaping it. Those events were the American invasion and occupation of Iraq, which began in 2003, and the Arab uprisings, which began in December 2010 (but whose roots stretch back much further).

Although the American invasion of Iraq resulted in the overthrow of the regime that had ruled over that long-suffering country, it brought chaos in its wake. It also brought a post-occupation government that neither ruled effectively nor won the support of much of the Iraqi population. Likewise, the giddiness that accompanied the early days of the Arab uprisings all too quickly soured in the prisons of Egypt and Bahrain and on the killing fields of Syria, Libya, and Yemen. Both events upset the regional order and unleashed mayhem—from state breakdown, inter-sectarian conflict, and the rise of the ultra-violent Islamic State in Iraq and Syria (also known as ISIS or, simply, the Islamic State), to proxy wars, humanitarian crises, and appalling displays of brutality. These misfortunes had either been held in check or had not existed before.

# 2

# THE ARAB UPRISINGS AND THEIR FALLOUT

## *How did the Arab uprisings begin?*

On December 17, 2010, a Tunisian street vendor, Muhammad Bouazizi, set himself on fire in front of the local government building in Sidi Bouzid, a town in central Tunisia. Earlier in the day, a policewoman had confiscated his wares and publicly humiliated him. He tried to complain at the local municipality, but to no avail. It was then that he went to a market and bought the flammable liquid with which he doused himself.

Bouazizi's act struck a chord among Tunisians, and protests quickly spread from Sidi Bouzid across the country. Tunisian protesters brought a number of issues to the table: unemployment, food inflation, corruption, poor living conditions, lack of freedoms, and lack of government responsiveness. The Tunisian General Labor Union (UGTT), the sometime lapdog of the regime, saw which way the wind was blowing and threw its support behind the protests. The UGTT had more than 600,000 members.

At first, Tunisian president Zine al-Abidine bin Ali, who had ruled for a quarter of a century, tried to pacify the protesters. In a pattern that was repeated time after time in the Arab world, he promised 300,000 new jobs, new parliamentary elections, and a "national dialogue." This did little to mollify them. On January 14, 2011—less than a month after

Bouazizi's self-immolation—military and political leaders decided enough was enough. With the army surrounding the presidential palace, bin Ali resigned and appointed his prime minister to head a caretaker government. Continued protests forced the appointment of another prime minister not as closely identified with the old regime. The uprising in Tunisia was the first ever in the modern Arab world to bring down an autocrat.

About a week and a half after bin Ali resigned, young people, many of whom belonged to the "April 6 Youth Movement," began their occupation of Tahrir Square in Cairo. (While Tahrir Square was but one site of many in Egypt where protests took place that day, it emerged as the symbolic center of the Egyptian uprising.) The April 6 Youth Movement got its name from a date in 2008 when young people, using Facebook, called for a general strike to support striking workers at a state-run textile factory. The general strike failed, giving lie to the miraculous powers frequently ascribed to Facebook and other social media by breathless Western commentators who, nevertheless, dubbed the 2010–2011 events in Tunisia and Egypt "Twitter Revolutions."

Unlike in 2008, protesters in 2011 were more successful. The security forces and goons-for-hire failed to dislodge them from the square. Then the army announced it would not fire on them. Strikes and anti-government protests spread throughout Egypt. On February 11, 2011, the army took matters into its own hands. It deposed President Hosni Mubarak and established a new government under the Supreme Council of the Armed Forces. This phase of the Egyptian uprising—what might be called the first street phase of the Egyptian uprising—was over in a mere eighteen days.

Soon after the Tunisian and Egyptian uprisings seemingly demonstrated what could be done, populations elsewhere began to smell blood in the water and followed suit. In spite of the obvious influence the first two uprisings had on those that followed, however, it would be wrong to view them through the lens of the first two. For example, after the outbreak of the Egyptian uprising, a similar protest movement emerged in Yemen. Nevertheless, it had very un-Tunisian, un-Egyptian results. As supporters of the regime squared off against social-networking youths and labor, along with military officers, disgruntled tribesmen, and opposition members of parliament whom the regime had failed to buy off, Yemen descended into chaos and violence. In the years that followed, Yemen suffered through extended periods of bloodshed intermittently interrupted by outside attempts to broker national reconciliation.

Uprisings in both Libya and Syria also turned into long, violent affairs. In Libya, dissidents called for a "Day of Rage" after the arrest of a prominent human-rights lawyer. He represented families of the 1,200 "disappeared" political prisoners whom the regime had murdered in cold blood in a single incident in 1996. As fighting between regime loyalists and regime opponents spread, NATO weighed in against the regime. This transformed a struggle that had begun as resistance to an oppressive regime into one pitting rival militias and warlords battling each other over power and turf. And after months of predictions that "it couldn't happen in Syria," it did. As in Libya, a spontaneous uprising in a town far from the capital sparked a seemingly endless and bloody antigovernment insurrection. However the Syrian uprising plays out, neither the Syrian people nor the villages and cities in which they live will ever return to their pre-uprising condition.

Protesters challenged monarchies as well. After protests modeled on those of Egypt broke out in Bahrain, the government struck back violently. Using the excuse that Iranian subversion was behind the protests, it invited in troops and police from neighboring Saudi Arabia and the UAE to help "restore order." A period of brutal repression followed. As in Libya, outside intervention determined the course of an uprising.

In Saudi Arabia and Morocco, kings who had presented themselves as "reformers" faced protesters who demanded expanded representation, an end to corruption, and constitutional checks on monarchic power. Significantly, protesters did not demand the replacement of the regime, as protesters elsewhere had done. Both governments sought to calm the waters by offering their citizens inducements. The Saudi government promised a $130 billion benefits package for its citizens. The Moroccan government agreed to superficial reforms.

These were the main sites of contention during the four months of what commentators have dubbed the "Arab Spring." There were other sites as well. There were also sites where populations took to the streets after the initial wave had crested. All told, since Bouazizi's suicide, protests or uprisings in one form or another have broken out in almost all of the twenty-two states that consider themselves part of the Arab world.

### How appropriate is the term "Arab Spring" to describe the uprisings?

There are two terms commonly used to describe what happened in the Arab world in 2010–2011. The first and most popular is "Arab Spring." This term might have seemed appropriate in the early, heady days of the uprisings. Today, however, it appears more ironic than descriptive. There are other problems with the term as well. For one, the uprisings were not entirely Arab. In Libya, for example, Berbers played an important role in toppling the regime. Nor can events in the Arab world during 2010–2011 be viewed as a discrete phenomenon that might be isolated within the span of a single "season." Not only did some uprisings continue in one form or another afterward, others began long after the arrival of the 2011 summer solstice. Furthermore, the so-called Arab Spring was not a unique event in Arab history; rather, it was but the latest phase in a three-decade-long struggle for human and democratic rights and social and economic justice in the region.

The second term commonly used to describe what has been happening in the Arab world since Bouazizi's death is "wave," as in a "revolutionary wave." There are pluses and minuses to viewing the uprisings as a wave. On the plus side, there is no denying that later Arab uprisings borrowed techniques of mobilization and symbols from earlier ones. Town squares that became the sites of protest throughout the Arab world were renamed "Tahrir," after the main site of protest in Cairo, and many uprisings began with a scheduled "Day of Rage," also borrowed from the Egyptian model. Then there is the highly touted use of social-networking sites for the purpose of mobilization, not to mention the common demands for human and democratic rights and social justice.

There are, however, two main objections to the use of the wave metaphor. Most significantly, the metaphor makes it seem that the spread of the uprisings and protests from state to state was inevitable, like a wave washing over a beach. Its use thus obscures the fact that the uprisings and protests spread as a result of tens of thousands of individual decisions made by participants who chose on a daily basis to face the full repressive power of their governments. The wave metaphor also obscures the fact that the goals and styles of the uprisings and protests have varied widely from country to country. The goal of some has been the complete overthrow of the regime, while the goal of others has been the reform of the regime. In some places, initial protests came about after meticulous preparation; in others, the spark was spontaneous. And there have been times when uprisings have been predominantly peaceful and other times when they took a violent turn.

Despite the metaphor's problems, thinking of the Arab uprisings in terms of a wave is useful if it is understood that what happened in the Arab world in 2010–2011 had not only a region-wide dimension but a local one as well. There were, of course, a number of factors that made it likely that an uprising in one or another place would find a sympathetic audience elsewhere in the region. Since the 1950s, for example, all Arab states came to share similar characteristics. And since the mid-1970s, all Arab states have faced similar conditions and shocks that have made them vulnerable to popular anger. Nevertheless, variations in local history, state structure, and state capability shaped the course of each uprising. Those variations made it impossible for Libyans, Yemenis, or Syrians, for example, to replicate the relative peacefulness and quick resolution which marked the initial phases of the Tunisian and Egyptian uprisings.

And there was an additional factor that shaped the path of a number of the uprisings: foreign intervention. States both outside and within the region had an interest in the outcomes of the various uprisings and acted accordingly. Some wanted one or another uprising to succeed, others, to fail. Indeed, in Libya, Yemen, Bahrain, Syria, and even Egypt, foreign assistance proved decisive for successes enjoyed by insurgents (Libya), counterinsurgents (Yemen, Bahrain, Egypt), or both (Syria).

### What deep-seated factors made Arab states vulnerable to popular anger?

Overall, there are five region-wide factors that made all states in the Arab world vulnerable to popular anger. Three of these were deep seated; two were contingent (that is, fortuitous and unpredictable). None of these factors actually *caused* the uprisings, per se. To attribute causation to these or any other factors overlooks a key variable—the human element—that determines whether an uprising will or will not occur. That Tunisians would connect a tragic death to the corruption and brutality of the regime that governed them, and then risk their lives to remove that regime, was not inevitable. People making choices in real time drove the uprisings.

The first long-term factor that made Arab states vulnerable to popular anger was neo-liberalism. When states adopted neo-liberal policies, they effectively tore up the "benefits for compliance" ruling bargain that had bound populations to their governments.

Neo-liberalism got its tentative start in the Arab world in December 1976, when Egypt negotiated a $450 million credit line with the IMF. In return, the Egyptian government pledged to cut commodity supports and direct subsidies. Over the next three decades, the IMF negotiated ever more expansive agreements with cash-strapped governments throughout the region. But by obeying the dictates of the IMF, governments encountered resistance from their populations. Those populations engaged in acts of defiance that ranged from revolt (so-called IMF riots) to labor activism.

Populations found two aspects of neo-liberalism particularly repellent. The first was the fraying of the social safety net and threats to middle-class welfare. Of particular concern were threats to across-the-board subsidies for food and fuel. At the recommendation of the IMF, those subsidies were replaced by subsidies targeted to those who lived in "extreme poverty." Populations also took a dim view of the sell-off of publicly owned enterprises to private entrepreneurs—a policy known as privatization. For many, privatization threatened state-employment guarantees. Furthermore, privatization did not lead, as its proponents promised, to free-market capitalism, but rather to crony capitalism, as regime loyalists took advantage of their access to the corridors of power. Privatization also widened the gulf between rich and poor. The worst of the crony capitalists thus came to symbolize systemic corruption in the buildup to the uprisings, and select crony capitalists heard their names chanted on the streets during them.

Accompanying the neo-liberal revolution was the so-called Human Rights Revolution, which began in the mid-1970s—the second factor that made states in the region vulnerable. The term "Human Rights Revolution" refers to two phenomena. First, it refers to a transformation of the notion of human rights. Before the 1970s, the words "human rights" referred to a breadbasket of rights: collective rights (such as the right of a nation to self-determination), economic rights (such as a person's right to a job), and individual rights (freedom of assembly, freedom from torture). After the revolution, the last meaning became predominant, particularly when used in international law. In addition, the term "Human Rights Revolution" refers to a time when governments (particularly in the West) and nongovernmental organizations alike put the rights of citizens on the international agenda.

It is no coincidence that the advance of neo-liberalism and the Human Rights Revolution took place simultaneously. Both privileged the rights of individuals over the rights of states or groups. Neo-liberalism did so in terms of individuals' economic rights; the Human Rights Revolution in terms of their political, civil, and personal rights. In theory, the two are interconnected. A free market depends on autonomous, rights-bearing individuals who need to be free to gather information, make decisions, and enter into voluntary associations with one another, whether on the floor of a stock exchange or in a town hall meeting (although the example of China demonstrates how governments might sanction such rights in the economic realm while denying them elsewhere). The United States found it useful to conjoin the two in its diplomatic endeavors. Together, they provided a comprehensive alternative to the collectivism and state-centrism of the Soviet Union and the newly assertive independent states of the postcolonial world.

The Arab world was not impervious to the Human Rights Revolution. A wide variety of individuals, from leftists and liberals to members of the loyal opposition and even Muslim clerics, found human rights to be an effective tool in the struggle against their autocratic governments. It was no accident, then, that the uprisings of 2010–2011 initially spoke in the language of human rights, as well as democratic rights, no matter how they evolved over time.

The third long-term factor that made Arab regimes vulnerable was their brittleness. The years between the onset of the economic crisis of 2008 and the Tunisian uprising were not good ones for governments throughout the world. Governments found themselves caught between bankers and economists recommending austerity, on the one hand, and populations fearing the end of the welfare state that provided for them, on the other. While uprisings were spreading in the Arab world, governments fell in the United Kingdom, Greece, Ireland, Portugal, Spain, Iceland, Italy, and elsewhere. Governments were challenged in France and the United States. Throughout it all, not one government was overthrown, nor were political institutions uprooted. Blame fell on politicians and parties and the policies they pushed.

In the Arab world, populations could not turn popular representatives out of office because there were no popular representatives. This is why populations throughout the region took to the streets as their first option. This also explains why the most common slogan during this period was "The people demand the downfall of the *nizam* [regime]," not "The people demand the downfall of the *hukuma* [government]."

### What contingent factors made Arab states vulnerable to popular anger?

In addition to the deep-seated factors that made Arab states vulnerable to popular anger, there were two contingent ones. The first of these was demography. In 2011, approximately 60 percent of the population of the Arab world was under the age of thirty. Even more telling was the percentage of youth between the ages of fifteen and twenty-nine, the period during which most enter the job market and compete on the marriage market. In 2010, youths between the ages of fifteen and twenty-nine made up 29 percent of the population of Tunisia, 30 percent of the population of Egypt, and 34 percent of the population of Libya. They also made up the bulk of the unemployed (in Egypt they made up 90 percent of the unemployed).

Demography is not, of course, destiny, and frustrations about job or life prospects do not necessarily translate into rebellion. Furthermore, youth was hardly the only segment of the Arab population that mobilized during the uprisings: In

Tunisia and Egypt, labor played a major role; in Libya and Syria, parents protesting the way the state had dealt with their children sparked them. Nevertheless, by 2010 there was a cohort of youths throughout the Arab world with a significant set of grievances. Under the proper circumstances, this cohort was available to be mobilized for oppositional politics.

The other contingent factor that made regimes in the Arab world vulnerable was a global rise in food prices. Between mid-2010 and January 2011, the world price of wheat, for example, more than doubled. Economists attribute this price rise to a number of factors, from speculation to drought to more acreage in the United States and Europe devoted to growing corn for biofuel.

The Arab Middle East is more dependent on imported food than is any other region in the world. At the time of its uprising, Egypt was the world's largest wheat importer. In addition to its dependence on food imports, however, there are two other reasons that skyrocketing food prices are a particular burden in the Arab world. First, the portion of household spending in 2010 that went to pay for food in the Arab world was as high as 63 percent in Morocco. Compare that to the average percentage of household spending that went to pay for food in the United States: 7 percent—a figure that includes eating as entertainment (that is, dining outside the home). The second reason skyrocketing food prices in the Arab world were particularly punishing is neo-liberalism. Pressure from the United States and the IMF has constrained governments from intervening into markets to fix prices and has forced governments to abandon across-the-board subsidies on food.

### What were the uprisings like in Tunisia and Egypt?

Once uprisings and protests began to break out in the region, they took a number of forms. In the main, they might be placed into five clusters: Tunisia and Egypt; Yemen and Libya; Bahrain and Syria; the monarchies; and Iraq, Lebanon, and Palestine.

Let us start with Tunisia and Egypt. During the uprisings in the two states, militaries stepped in to depose long-ruling autocrats who faced widespread disaffection. The militaries thus cut the revolutionary process short. This prevented a thorough housecleaning in both places.

Tunisia and Egypt are unique in the Arab world. Beginning in the nineteenth century, both experienced two centuries of continuous state-building. As a result, in both there were long-lived, functioning institutions autonomous from (although subservient to) the executive branch of the government. The military was one of those institutions, but there were others as well, including the judiciary and security services. Together, these institutions make up what political scientists call the "deep state." When faced with an unprecedented crisis, the institutions of the deep state closed ranks to protect the old order.

The struggle between the deep state and the forces promoting change in Tunisia and Egypt defined the course of the two uprisings. When moderate Islamist organizations—Ennahda in Tunisia, the Muslim Brotherhood in Egypt—won popular mandates to form governments at the conclusion of the initial phase of the uprisings, the deep state joined forces with remnants of the old regime and more secular-oriented groups within the population in defiance. In Egypt, the brotherhood saw itself locked in a battle to the death with its adversaries, which felt likewise. It therefore refused to share power with them, and even pushed through a constitution it drafted when it appeared that the judiciary was about to dissolve the constitutional assembly on procedural grounds. As the crisis escalated—and as the Egyptian economy went into a free fall—hundreds of thousands of Egyptians once again took to the streets.

As had happened in 2011, the military, now under Commander in Chief Abdel Fattah el-Sisi, stepped in. Saudi Arabia, the UAE, and Kuwait, opposed to Muslim Brotherhood rule anywhere, gave financial backing to the coup. Sisi dissolved the brotherhood, had a new constitution drafted which enhanced the power of the deep state, and established a regime far more repressive than Mubarak's. According to the Egyptian Centre for Economic and Social Rights, during the first four months following its takeover, the military killed 2,665 of their fellow citizens, wounded 16,000, and arrested 13,145.[1]

The uprising in Tunisia took a different path but has ended up in a similar place to the uprising in Egypt. Unlike the Egyptian Muslim Brotherhood, Ennahda did not overplay its hand. From the beginning, in fact, Ennahda reached out to opposition parties and brought them into the government. And when faced with the same crises and oppositional forces faced by the Egyptian Muslim Brotherhood, Ennahda, as well as its opponents, stepped away from the precipice. Ennahda dissolved the government it dominated and called for new elections (which it lost). It also agreed to the most liberal constitution in the Arab world. That constitution did not refer to Islamic law at all, and it promised women the same number of seats as men in all elected bodies.

Ultimately, however, the Tunisian uprising was not able to avoid the pitfalls that befell other uprisings. In 2019, after years in which Tunisians were unable to gain the "bread, jobs, dignity" they had demanded in the heady days of the revolution, they elected a populist political novice, Kais Saied, president. Saied, a former constitutional law professor, promised to end the political gridlock and economic stagnation that unmade the promise of the uprising. Instead, he set about unraveling Tunisia's hard-won constitutional order. He suspended parliament and dismissed the prime minister, dissolved the Supreme Judicial Council, jailed political opponents, appointed a commission to rewrite the constitution, and declared his intention to rule by decree.

Saied's defenders claimed he merely wants to transform Tunisia's British-style parliamentary system into a French-style presidential system run by an activist-but-democratically-elected president. His detractors, on the other hand, see expanding authoritarianism. Whatever the case, the democratic gains Tunisians experienced in the aftermath of their uprising have all but disappeared.

### Why have Islamic movements been so popular in the Middle East?

The terms "Islamism" and "Islamic movements" embrace a grab bag of associations, parties, and governments that seek to order their societies according to what they consider to be Islamic principles. The term "Islamist" refers to those who profess those principles. Some Islamists choose to participate in politics to achieve this end; others do not. Some use violence to achieve their goals; others have participated in the political process. Some believe that Islamic principles provide them with a strict road map to be followed without deviation; others treat those principles more gingerly. Hence the attempt by some Islamists to meld human rights and democracy with Islamic principles.

Islamist parties won the first free elections in Tunisia and Egypt. They have done well elsewhere, such as in Yemen, Morocco, Algeria, Palestine, and Jordan. This begs the question: "Why?"

It is commonplace to treat Islamist movements as a special category of political movement. This is because the goals of Islamist movements—establishing regimes that observe and enforce Islamic law, for example—differ from the goals of other political movements. But rather than focusing on the distinctive goals of Islamist movements, we might do better to understand them within a comparative framework. This would make Islamist movements (and those who follow them) appear less idiosyncratic and explain their appeal.

In the main, there have been four possible foundations for social and political movements in the modern Middle East, as elsewhere in the contemporary world: utopianism, demands for the restoration or expansion of rights, nativism, or some combination thereof. The category of utopianism includes Marxist and anarchist movements—movements that seek to create a world that does not yet exist. While most Marxists and anarchists have a road map for what they seek to accomplish (*Das Kapital*, for example), they do not have much nostalgia for the past. Conversely, those who make demands for rights—be they for social and economic justice or for collective or individual rights—do not want to abolish the current order; they want to reform it or join it on an equal footing. All the uprisings that took place in the Arab world in 2010–2011 made claims for rights.

Then there are nativist movements. Nativists believe that the only means to bring about the regeneration of a particular community is for that community to embrace its authentic, defining traditions. Like movements based on the demand for rights, nativist movements are commonplace in the modern world. For example, nativism provides the ideological foundation for the Hindu nationalist party in India, the Bharatiya Janata Party, as well as for the slogan "Make America great again." And they are popular, as can be seen from their current resurgence worldwide. The only thing that makes nativism in the Islamic world different from nativism elsewhere is that Islam can be mobilized to play a role in defining authenticity there.

Some social and political movements have been exclusively nativist or rights-based. Wahhabism (the official ideology of Saudi Arabia) is exclusively nativist. Its followers advocate returning to the Islam they believe Muhammad and the first Islamic community practiced.

Wahhabism is a form of salafism. Salafism refers to a technique some Muslims use for discovering religious truth. Salafis believe they can rely on only two sources to get at that truth: the Qur'an (which, for Muslims, is an emanation from God), and the sayings and acts of the prophet Muhammad and his seventh-century companions. As a result, all salafis are nativists, whether they choose to participate in politics (like ISIS and the Taliban in Afghanistan), or not.

On the other hand, contemporary labor activism and consumer boycotts usually speak the language of economic justice without appeals to tradition. So did the IMF riots that spread throughout the region in the 1980s.

Most modern social and political movements, however, have combined nativism with an appeal to rights. The few remaining stateless nationalities in the region—the Palestinians, the Kurds, the Sahrawis in southern Morocco—certainly do. So do all nationalists, who claim a right to self-determination based on a distinct linguistic, ethnic, religious, or historical tradition. Likewise, other groups. For example, in 1980 the Berber community of Algeria mounted protests demanding the government in Algiers recognize their collective right to maintain their Berber identity and language, Tamazight. In other words, the so-called Berber Spring claimed the right for Algerian Berbers to maintain their traditions. And the various Islamists and Islamist groups that, at various times, embraced the platform of human rights, democratic participation, or both—including the Muslim Brotherhood of Egypt and Ennahda—have combined nativism with a demand for rights as well.

### Why did uprisings in Yemen and Libya differ from those in Tunisia and Egypt?

Tunisia and Egypt had a long history of state construction and institutional development. Among those institutions was the military, which stepped in during the uprisings to prevent the complete elimination of the old regime. It did this by sending the most visible symbol of that regime—Ben Ali in the case of Tunisia, Mubarak in the case of Egypt—packing. This scenario was impossible in the cases of Yemen and Libya, because no unified and autonomous military, replete with a functioning chain of command and esprit de corps, existed in either. And while there was no institutionalized deep state to push back against the new regime in Yemen and Libya as there was in Tunisia and Egypt, there was no functioning administrative apparatus either that would have made the post-uprising transition smoother. In both Yemen and Libya, regimes fragmented, pitting the officers and soldiers, cabinet ministers, politicians, and diplomats who stood with the regime against those who joined the opposition.

The fragmentation of regimes in the two states is not surprising: In contrast to Tunisia and Egypt, both Yemen and Libya are poster children for what political scientists call "weak states." In weak states, governments and the bureaucracies upon which they depend are unable to assert their authority over the entirety of the territory they rule. Nor are they able to extend their reach beneath the surface of society. It is partly for this reason that populations in weak states lack strong national identities and allegiances. Such is the situation in both Yemen and Libya.

To a certain extent, the weakness of the Yemeni and Libyan states came about as a result of geography. Neither country has terrain that makes it easy to govern—Yemen because of the roughness of its terrain, Libya because of the terrain's expansiveness. To a certain extent, the weakness of the Yemeni and Libyan states is a result of their history (or lack thereof). Both states are relatively recent creations that combine disparate territories and populations. Yemen had been divided between an independent North Yemen and South Yemen until 1990. Contrasting social structures found in each Yemen reflect the legacies of formal imperialism in the south and the absence of formal imperialism in the north. The United Nations created an independent federated Libya in 1952 from the remnants of three former Italian colonies which had been kept separate until 1934. Even then, regional differences remained.

The final reason for the weakness of the Yemeni and Libyan states was the ruling styles of their leaders. Both President Ali Abdullah Saleh of Yemen, who ruled Yemen since its founding in 1990, and Muammar Qaddafi of Libya, who took power in 1969, purposely avoided establishing strong institutions. Instead, they favored a personalistic style of rule. This gave them more leeway in playing off tribes and other internal groupings against one another.

The weakness of state institutions caused their collapse once uprisings gained momentum. As a result, uprisings in both states were both violent and long and invited foreign meddling.

### How could regimes in Bahrain and Syria hold on so doggedly?

Unlike Tunisia and Egypt, where one faction in the ruling elite turned on another, and unlike Yemen and Libya, where regimes splintered as a result of the shock of the uprisings there, regimes in Syria and Bahrain maintained their cohesion against the uprisings. One might even say that in Syria and Bahrain regimes had no choice but to maintain their cohesion against uprisings: Rulers of both states effectively "coup-proofed"[2] their regimes by, among other things, exploiting ties of sect and kinship to build a close-knit, interdependent ruling group.

The ruling group in Syria consists of President Bashar al-Assad, his extended family, and members of the minority Alawite community (which makes up anywhere from 12 to 17 percent of the Syrian population, depending on whom you ask). When the uprising began, President Bashar al-Assad's cousin was the head of the presidential guard, his brother was commander of the Republican Guard and Fourth Armored Division, and his now deceased brother-in-law was deputy chief of staff. None of them could have turned on the regime. If the regime went, they would go, too. As a matter of fact, few persons of note defected from the regime and, of those who have—one brigadier general, a prime minister (which in Syria is a post of little importance), and an ambassador to Iraq—not one was Alawite.

The core of the regime in Bahrain consists of members of the ruling Khalifa family, who hold critical cabinet portfolios. At the time of the uprising, these ranged from the office of prime minister and deputy prime minister to ministers of defense, foreign affairs, finance, and national security. The commander of the army and commander of the royal guard were also family. Members of the minority Sunni community, who make up an estimated 30 to 40 percent of the population, form the main pillar and primary constituency of the regime.

Although the uprising started out as nonsectarian in nature (as had Syria's), the Bahraini regime deliberately sectarianized it (as the Syrian regime did). The regime responded to a movement that demanded social justice, human rights, and democratization as if it were one that wanted nothing more than Shi'i supremacy at the expense of Sunnis. As a result, members of the Sunni community circled their wagons in its defense.

Foreign intervention has played a critical role in determining the course of the uprisings in both Bahrain and Syria. The Saudi and Emirati soldiers and policemen who crossed the causeway linking Bahrain's main island with the mainland took up positions throughout the capital, Manama. This freed up the Bahraini military and security services (led by members of the ruling family and made up of Sunnis from Pakistan, Jordan, and elsewhere) to crush the opposition.

Having suppressed the uprising, the regime then embarked on a campaign of repression which was harsh by even Gulf standards. Regime opponents have faced mass arrests and torture in prison, demonstrations are banned, and insulting the king can result in a prison sentence of up to seven years. Security forces armed with riot gear have cordoned off rebellious Shi'i villages, terrorizing residents with nighttime raids. It is also illegal to possess a Guy Fawkes mask, the accessory of choice of anarchists and members of Occupy movements, like Occupy Wall Street, the world over. All the while, the regime hid behind the façade of a series of national dialogues whose outcomes it fixed.

While foreign intervention helped curtail the Bahraini uprising, it had the opposite effect in Syria. Iran, Russia, and Hizbullah have supported the regime. The West, Saudi Arabia, Qatar, Turkey, the opposition. Both sides have funneled arms and money to their proxies. Hizbullah fighters, Iranian soldiers, and Russian airmen and Special Forces have also joined the fray. This has not only served to escalate the violence, it created the environment in which ISIS could incubate before it set out to create its caliphate from portions of Iraq and Syria.

### Why did the uprisings leave most Arab monarchies relatively unscathed?

There were no uprisings of significance in Qatar and the UAE. Those that broke out in the four of the seven remaining monarchies—Morocco, Saudi Arabia, Kuwait, and Oman— were never as regime threatening as those that broke out elsewhere. With the exception of the uprising in Bahrain (and, perhaps, Jordan), *protests* in the Arab monarchies share two important characteristics that set them apart from *uprisings* in the Arab republics: They have, for the most part, been more limited in scope, and they have demanded reform of the regime, not its overthrow.

It is not altogether clear why this discrepancy has been the case. Nor, for that matter, is it clear whether it will continue to be so. Some political scientists have argued that the reason the demand in monarchies has been for reform and not revolution is that monarchs have an ability that presidents—even presidents for life—do not have: They can retain executive power while ceding legislative power to an elected assembly and prime minister. As a result, the assembly and prime minister, not the monarch, become the focal point of popular anger when things go wrong. Unfortunately, this explanation rings hollow. While it might hold true for Kuwait, which has a parliament that can be, at times, quite raucous, Saudi Arabia does not even have a parliament and the king *is* the prime minister.

Others argue that oil wealth enables monarchs to buy off their opposition or prevent an opposition from arising in the first place. This might explain what happened in the Gulf monarchies, but Morocco (which had an uprising that the king enfeebled with a few cosmetic reforms) does not have oil. On the other hand, Bahrain—which has had a long history of rebellion and had a full-fledged uprising in 2011—is, when compared with Morocco, hydrocarbon rich.

It is entirely possible that in the future it will be necessary to reassess whether a monarchic category even exists. Bahrain was not the only monarchy in which opposition leaders called for the removal of the king. The same occurred in Jordan during demonstrations in November 2012. Although those demonstrations soon ran out of steam, there is no way to determine how deep the sentiment runs or whether it might re-emerge in the future. And while the world was focused on the anemic demonstrations of social-networking youths in Saudi Arabia's capital, violent protests, which met with violent repression, broke out in the predominantly Shi'i Eastern Province of the country. Taking these latter protests into account challenges the notion that protests in the monarchies were limited in scope. Ultimately, the small number of monarchies included in this category (four out of eight in the region) makes any conclusions about a monarchic exception problematic.

### What were protests in hybrid regimes like?

Iraq, Lebanon, and Palestine had a democratic façade when their protests broke out. The characteristics and objectives of the uprisings in all three reflected this. For example, populations had relative freedom to mass on the streets (often alongside disgruntled members of the ruling elite) and demand accountability from dysfunctional elected governments. Protests unfolded over time. And as governments proved unable or unwilling to break the political gridlock and answer even the most rudimentary needs of their populations, those populations expanded their demands to include an overhaul of the entire political system.

Demonstrations that began throughout Iraq on February 25, 2011, protested the lack of potable water, electrical shortages, and high unemployment. They then morphed into demonstrations that demanded the removal of oligarchs and an end to the sectarian system that guaranteed places in government based on sectarian identity. Weekly protests continued in Baghdad for years afterward. Demonstrations held in Beirut, Lebanon, four and a half years later protested the government's inability to remove garbage or provide other services (which secured for the campaign its evocative name, the "You Stink" movement). It followed a trajectory similar to the protest movement in Iraq. Neither movement has, to date, been able to remove or even move entrenched politicians.

A separate protest movement in Iraq began in winter 2014 in the Sunni areas of the country. Protesters demanded the end of discriminatory policies against their community perpetrated by the Shiʻi government that the Americans had left behind after their withdrawal. The government met those protests with extreme violence (as it did the initial protests). This encouraged many Sunnis to sit on their hands or openly support ISIS when it began its conquests.

The Palestinian uprising took place in several stages. In January 2011, a group calling itself "Gaza Youth Breaks Out" issued its first manifesto, which stated, "There is a revolution growing inside of us, an immense dissatisfaction and frustration that will destroy us unless we find a way of canalizing this energy into something that can challenge the status quo and give us some kind of hope."[3]

That energy was "canalized" through the March 15 Youth Movement, a loose association of social-media-savvy young people similar to Egypt's April 6 Youth Movement. Like its predecessor, the March 15 Youth Movement began its protests with a "Day of Rage" in which tens of thousands of Palestinians took part. Rather than demand the ouster of the regime as their

Egyptian counterparts had done, however, movement leaders demanded reconciliation between the two rival governments that ruled the West Bank and Gaza, respectively.

The final stage of the Palestinian uprising took place in the West Bank in September 2012 after the government raised prices on food and fuel. Spurred on by the same sort of labor activism that had proved decisive in the Egyptian uprising, protesters soon escalated their demands from the economic to the political: They called for the dismissal of the prime minister who led the West Bank government, the dismantling of that government, and the establishment of a Palestinian state with East Jerusalem as its capital, among other demands. The protest deeply shook the Palestinian leadership. It was then that it decided to seize the initiative and assuage public opinion by taking the case for Palestinian statehood to the General Assembly of the United Nations.

### Were the Arab uprisings bound to fail?

For anyone watching the Egyptian uprising, it was difficult not to get caught up in the moment. Nevertheless, it is not unreasonable to ask how anyone could have thought that a regime as strong as the Egyptian—with its entrenched institutions and powerbrokers, its far-ranging patronage networks, its anti-democratic and oil-rich allies, its one-million-man army (including reserves) and two-million-man security apparatus—would throw in the towel after eighteen days without putting up more of a fight. This might be asked of other, less powerful regimes, as well.

From the beginning, protesters and rebels throughout the Arab world faced overwhelming odds, the tenacity of ruling cliques fighting for their lives, the hostility of those dependent on the old order, foreign intervention, lack of foreign intervention, and extremist groups out for their own ends. Since participants in the uprisings were, more often than not, united by what they were against—the regime—rather than what they were for, they also disagreed among themselves about goals. In all cases but that of Libya (and, to a far lesser extent, Syria), they faced the indifference or hostility of the United States. Finally, the very spontaneity, leaderlessness, diversity, and loose organization on which the uprisings thrived proved to be their Achilles heel. True, these attributes kept regimes off balance and prevented them from reining in rebellious activity. But they also prevented protesters and rebels from agreeing on and implementing common tactics, strategy, and program.

There is one further factor that might have doomed the protests and uprisings to failure even had they been able to upturn or overthrow the old order: the wretched state of the economies of the non-oil-producing states and the absence of a blueprint other than the widely hated neo-liberalism to fix them. Throughout the region, economies went from bad to worse after uprisings broke out. This was the result of interrupted production, strikes, a lack of security that discouraged commerce and tourism, damage to infrastructure and sites of production, and displacement and migration.

In 2013, hundreds of thousands of Egyptians, angered by fuel shortages, electricity blackouts, and higher food prices, went out on the streets to demand that the incompetent but democratically elected president leave office. Most cheered on as the army first gave him an ultimatum, then arrested him and assumed power. Egypt's short-lived experiment in democracy had come to an end.

Writing of revolutions, the Italian communist theorist Antonio Gramsci differentiated between a "war of maneuver" and a "war of position." A war of maneuver is a direct confrontation between the old order and those opposing it, as took place during the Russian Revolution. A war of position is the slow, meticulous winning over of a population to one's ideas by infiltrating institutions and structures such as the press, trade unions, civic associations, and the like, so that those committed to change have already created the foundations of a counter-society by the time they assume power. In the case of the Arab uprisings, protesters fought a war of maneuver, not a war of position. As a result, "deep states" were able to regroup, call on outside support, and stigmatize and isolate their oppositions. And as a result, throughout the region the forces of counter-revolution could claim victory over the forces of change.

### What were the overall effects of the uprisings that began in 2010–2011?

To date, the scorecard for the uprisings that began in 2010 is disheartening. In Egypt and all the monarchies, the forces of re-action snuffed out the demands for change. Although the state system as a whole is not threatened—thanks in large measure to the support of both great and regional powers for the status quo—it is unlikely that the inhabitants of Libya, Yemen, and Syria will live under functioning governments that rule over the entirety of their territories anytime soon.

Across the region, there has been a rise in sectarianism, fu-eled by a combination of the Syrian civil war, the Iranian-Saudi rivalry over which regional power would determine the fate of embattled regimes and the regional order, and the Islamic State's war on everyone—including Shi'is—who does not follow the group's rigid interpretation of Islam or bow to its will. And however much protesters in Lebanon and Iraq might aspire to end sectarianism, once people have segregated them-selves among "their own kind," or representation or employ-ment opportunities have been allocated according to religious affiliation, sectarianism is unlikely to disappear.

Foreign intervention has taken place with impunity, perhaps signaling the beginning of an epochal shift in the meaning of sovereignty and sovereign relations in the region. Petro-states like Saudi Arabia and the UAE, regional powers like Turkey and Iran, outside powers like the United States and Russia felt no compunction advancing their own interests on other nations' soil. Even Israel got into the act, attacking Iranian military units and facilities in Syria to underscore its red lines. Such intervention decisively shifted the trajectory of uprisings in Bahrain, Yemen, Syria, Libya, and Egypt.

In some states—Egypt, Bahrain, and much of the Arabian Peninsula—populations face the heavier hand of regimes that, for a brief moment, had caught a glimpse of their own mortality. Elsewhere—Syria, Libya, Yemen, Iraq, even Tunisia and the Sinai—the weakening of regimes or the diversion of their attention elsewhere created an environment in which violent Islamist groups, from ISIS and al-Qaeda to Syria's Ahrar al-Sham and al-Qaeda affiliate Jabhat al-Nusra, might breed. Again, the Saudi-Iranian competition has made matters worse. In their efforts to combat the expansion of Iranian influence in the region and uphold Sunni dominance in the Arab world, Saudi Arabia and its Gulf allies have supported a number of violent Islamist groups on the battlefields of Syria and elsewhere. They have also financed mosques and schools that spread doctrines similar to those espoused by violent Islamists, thus normalizing those doctrines.

Since 2011, the region has experienced one humanitarian crisis after another. In the most brutal war zones—Syria, Libya, Yemen, Iraq—entire towns and cities have been laid waste, their populations scattered. War and civil disorder have not only taken their toll in terms of civilian casualties, but have also destroyed billions of dollars of infrastructure and created a public health nightmare. And particularly in Syria and Yemen, mass starvation—both a consequence and an intentional tool of war—is an ongoing threat, endangering millions.

### Was there an "Arab Spring 2.0"?

Beginning in early 2018, protests once again broke out throughout the Arab world, from Morocco in the west to Iraq in the east. Among the other states affected were Tunisia, Jordan, Sudan, Algeria, Palestine, Egypt, Lebanon, Oman, and Syria (!). Pundits called this wave of protests "Arab Spring 2.0," a title taken from computer software marketing designating a new and improved product.

Local factors contributed to both the grievances and demands of the protesters. In Algeria, for example, protests erupted when the ailing president announced his "candidacy" for a fifth term. After the military turned on him, he stepped down. In Lebanon, protests over the introduction of new taxes morphed into a sustained movement against both a political class widely seen as corrupt and the sectarian political system. And in Morocco, protests over a stagnant economy and income inequality took on new life after the government introduced a mandatory "vaccine pass" for travel and access to most public venues in an attempt to halt the spread of COVID-19.

Underlying the protests, however, was a familiar litany of complaints. They included lack of governmental accountability, arbitrary rule, corruption, and mismanagement. This was, of course, to be expected, considering the failure of the protests and uprisings of 2010–2011 to achieve their aims. But what distinguished this wave of protests was the prominent role played by economic grievances in so many of them. Among those grievances were austerity budgets, poverty, new taxes, lack of government investment in infrastructure, higher costs for government-provided essentials such as electricity, and cuts in government-funded subsidies. These policies were, in large measure, the result of new rounds of neo-liberal economic reform, undertaken at the behest of creditors, the most prominent of which was the IMF.

Although bread-and-butter issues *did* play an important role in the uprisings and protests of 2010–2011, there is another reason to discard the idea of a "new and improved" wave of popular rebellion. That reason is that the phrase "Arab Spring 2.0" implies an "Arab Spring 1.0" that began in December 2010 with the self-immolation of Muhammad Bouazizi and ended with the onset of the Syrian uprising in March 2011. That is not the case. Rather, popular mobilization in the Arab world for human and democratic rights and social and economic justice began in the 1980s and has continued episodically ever since.

The demand for human rights lay at the heart of the "Berber Spring" of 1980, the fight by Algeria's largest ethnic minority for its rights. Eight years later, the Algerian "Black October" riots led to the first democratic elections in the Arab world (unfortunately, the government overturned their results). The Bahraini *intifada* of 1994–1999 began with a petition signed by one-tenth of Bahrain's inhabitants demanding an end to emergency rule, the restoration of rights revoked by that rule, release of political prisoners, pardons for political exiles, and the expansion of the franchise to women (*intifada* is Arabic for "shaking off," and is now commonly used to mean "rebellion"). Petitioners also demanded a restoration of the 1973 constitution, which provided for a parliament in which two-thirds of the members were to be elected.

The death of Syrian dictator Hafez al-Assad in 2000 spawned the rise of political salons throughout Syria. Participants in those salons expanded their movement through the circulation of the "Statement of the Ninety-Nine," then the "Statement of a Thousand," which echoed many of the same demands made during the Bahraini intifada, along with demands for multiparty elections and freedom of speech, assembly, and expression. Even after the "Damascus Spring" turned into the "Damascus Winter," aftershocks of the mobilization continued. Among those aftershocks was the Damascus Declaration Movement of 2005, which (initially) united the secular and religious opposition in a common demand for democratic rights.

These movements were only the tip of the iceberg. Following the spread of the pro-democracy *diwaniyya* (civic council) movement in the wake of the expulsion of Iraqi troops from Kuwait in 1991, Kuwait experienced two "color revolutions." The first—the "Blue Revolution"—lasted from 2002 to 2005. It won for Kuwaiti women the right to vote. A year later, Kuwaitis organized the "Orange Revolution" to promote electoral reform. In 2004, secular and Islamist Egyptians banded to form a group called "Kefaya" ("Enough"), which called on Mubarak to resign. In Morocco, popular agitation led to the establishment of the Equity and Reconciliation Commission in 2004 to investigate human-rights abuses that had occurred during the previous thirty years—the so-called Years of Lead. Lebanese took to the streets in 2005 in their Cedar Revolution, demanding the withdrawal of Syrian forces from that unfortunate country and parliamentary elections free from Syrian interference. In 2004, 2008, and 2010 Kurdish citizens protested for minority rights in Syria. And the list goes on.

Alongside these protests and uprisings for human rights and democratic governance were protests and uprisings for social and economic justice. Beginning in the late 1970s with IMF riots, this agitation continued through a six-month general strike in the Gafsa phosphate-mining region of Tunisia in 2008 and the surge of Egyptian labor activism from 2004 through 2010. During that period of activism, two million Egyptian workers and their families participated in more than 3,000 strikes, sit-ins, and walkouts. Sometimes protesters framed their demands in class terms; at other times, they framed them in human rights terms, as in the 2011 Tunisian slogan "A job is a right."

The events of 2010–2011 and those that have taken place since 2018 are not discrete events; rather, it would be better to view them as episodes within a continuum. And as events since 2018 have demonstrated, that continuum remains open-ended.

# 3

# THINGS FALL APART

## What is a "crisis state"?

According to the Crisis States Research Centre at the London School of Economics, "a crisis state is a state under acute stress, where reigning institutions face serious contestation and are potentially unable to manage conflict and shocks."[1] Like many such definitions, this one may seem a bit loose and arbitrary. It does, however, provide a useful starting point to describe a phenomenon endemic to the New Middle East.

Crisis states emerged in the New Middle East in a number of ways. Conflicts in Syria and Libya began similarly, with spontaneous uprisings that spread from provincial areas during the 2010–2011 wave of uprisings. Conflict in Yemen began as a result of dissatisfaction with international attempts to impose a settlement after the 2011 uprising there. Conflict in Iraq can be traced to the sectarianization of the country that followed the American invasion and occupation in 2003. The emergence of ISIS was both a catalyst for and a result of that sectarianization. The state it founded threatened not only the sovereignty and territorial integrity of Iraq, but Syria and states elsewhere. Finally, in Lebanon the economy went into a free fall, taking with it any semblance of a functioning state—a result of corruption and a political system that sustained that corruption.

## How did the conflict in Syria begin?

In the first week of March 2011, Syrian security forces arrested ten schoolchildren aged fifteen or younger in the dusty provincial city of Daraa. The arrest came after the agents caught them writing "Down with the regime [*nizam*]"—a slogan borrowed from the Egyptian uprising—on a wall. The children were imprisoned, and while in prison they were tortured. For about two weeks their families attempted to gain their release. Then they took to the streets. Security forces opened fire, killing several. The next day, their funeral procession brought out 20,000 demonstrators—in a city of 77,000—who chanted antigovernment slogans and attacked government buildings.

Coincidentally, protests erupted in the northern city of Banias on the same day the anguished parents went out on the streets in Daraa. As in the case of the Daraa protests, the protests in Banias initially reflected local concerns: the secular regime had transferred female schoolteachers there who wore the niqab, the Syrian variant of the veil, to administrative jobs. Then, like their compatriots in Daraa, protesters expanded their focus to national issues. These included the brutality of the regime, the absence of democratic institutions, and corruption.

Protests soon spread to the coastal city of Latakia, then to Duma, north of the capital. Protesters aired similar grievances and met with the same violence. In village after village, town after town, protesters took to the streets as word spread of their neighbors' boldness and the regime's response. Eventually, protests reached the suburbs of Damascus and Syria's largest city, Aleppo.

## Why did the Syrian conflict evolve as it did?

Three factors determined the course of the Syrian conflict. First, the regime of Bashar al-Assad responded to the uprising with military force. This was not initially the case: at the outset of the uprising, the regime treated it as a police matter and depended on the security services to put it down. While the security services did put down isolated pockets of resistance, however, they could not prevent protests from leapfrogging from quarter to quarter, town to town. Beginning in January 2012, the regime handed counterinsurgency to the army. The test case proved to be the district of Baba Amr in the city of Homs, which called itself the capital of the revolution. The army used all the firepower it could deploy—from tanks, helicopter gunships, and artillery to mortars, heavy machine guns, and snipers. It first cut off the city from the outside world, then softened up the rebel stronghold, reducing much of it to rubble. Finally, the army stormed the district, killing about 250 rebels and driving the remainder out.

Its mission a success, the military began applying the same tactics elsewhere, escalating the level of violence with the occasional use of poison gas and barrel bombs (barrels filled with TNT dropped from the air indiscriminately). It pummeled neighborhoods with artillery, barrel bombs, etc., then stormed them.

The government's new tactics had an unintended consequence, however: it changed the nature of the opposition. At the outset, protests had been localized and, in large measure, peaceful affairs. To protect demonstrations from snipers and informants, protesters staged rallies at night. Organized militias, made up of local fighters who had deserted from the Syrian army, provided further protection. With their communities under siege or bombardment, local militias were often forced to retreat from their own neighborhoods and regroup and fight wherever they sensed regime vulnerability. This was the origin of the "Free Syrian Army," the militia backed by the United States and much of the West. But the separation of the militias from their home turf strained the connection between the local militias and their civilian counterparts. Civilians lost control of the uprising, and the balance of power within the opposition tipped in favor of the fighters.

The second factor that determined the course of the Syrian conflict was that the regime transformed it into a sectarian conflict; that is, a conflict in which an individual's religious affiliation became the basis for their political allegiance.

The uprising had begun without reference to the diversity of religious communities that made up Syria; rather, protesters focused on the removal of a regime they considered repressive and corrupt. The fact that the uprising transcended religious affiliation is hardly surprising. Before the uprising Syrian society as a whole was not divided along sectarian lines. Members of sects of course recognized their religious differences and, in the privacy of their homes, might have made derogatory comments about one another. But they mingled with members of other sects in markets, public schools (where they all wore the same uniforms), coffee shops, and on public transportation. To divide the opposition, the regime deliberately set out to polarize Syrian society—and the uprising—into opposing sectarian camps.

The regime adopted a number of tactics to accomplish this. As soon as the uprising broke out, it identified the opposition not in political terms but in religious ones. By doing so, the predominantly Alawite regime was able to foster fear among fellow non-Sunnis that the overthrow of the regime would have horrendous consequences for them. The regime labeled its opponents salafis, Islamists, terrorists, jihadis, and agents of Saudi Arabia. (The term "jihadi," in its current usage, refers to a Sunni Muslim committed to waging violent *jihad*, or struggle, against non-Muslims or those they consider non-Muslim. Jihadis, always violent, are a variety of Islamist, frequently non-violent.) To ensure this would be a self-fulfilling prophecy, as early as spring 2011 the regime released salafis, Islamists, and jihadis, including those associated with al-Qaeda, from prison. Many ended up in the on-and-off al-Qaeda affiliate in Syria, Jabhat al-Nusra, or in ISIS.

The regime also used violence to sectarianize society. It organized armed "popular committees" to protect Alawite villages. It also equipped pro-regime vigilantes with knives and clubs for use in street battles with mostly unarmed protesters. And it used the shabiha (a name probably derived from the Arabic word for "ghosts")—Alawite thugs who hailed from Assad's hometown and its immediate vicinity—to provoke tit-for-tat violence against Sunnis. In July 2011, nine died in Homs after an Alawite mob surrounded a Sunni mosque in one of the first recorded instances of sectarian conflict during the uprising. That was just a harbinger of worse to come: in Baida and Banias, for example, shabiha massacred 248 Sunnis. In the village of Aqrab, opposition fighters slaughtered at least 125 Alawites.

The efforts of the government to sectarianize the conflict paid off. Unlike in Libya, in Syria the cost of regime fragmentation or collapse proved too high for both the regime's inner circle and its supporters, a large number of whom came from minority communities. They believed they had no choice but to rally around their purported defender. For them, it was more than a matter of political preference; the question at hand had become one of survival.

The final factor that determined the course of the Syrian conflict was the intervention of outside powers in support of the regime or the opposition. Iran, Hezbollah, and Russia intervened on the side of the Syrian government. The West, Saudi Arabia and the Gulf states, and Turkey on the side of the opposition. For the most part, intervention on behalf of the regime was both indirect and direct. Intervention on behalf of the opposition was mainly channeled through the various militias outside powers believed best served their interests. Saudi Arabia and the Gulf states worked with Islamist militias, the United States and the West with more secular ones.

Foreign intervention ultimately affected the course of the war and narrowed the field of possible outcomes. At the beginning of 2015, the Syrian civil war was, according to *The New York Times*, a "chaotic stalemate."[2] Neither the government nor the opposition forces arrayed against it was able to gain the upper hand. Battlefield gains were reversed, regained, then reversed again. Battles fought between the two sides more closely resembled a war of attrition than a war of movement.

By the summer of that same year, however, the situation on the battlefield had completely shifted in the rebels' favor. In 2014, the United States, Jordan, and Saudi Arabia set up a joint Military Operations Command (MOC) in Amman, Jordan. Commonly known as the "operations room," MOC collected intelligence, financial and logistical assistance, and military know-how from the United States and Saudi Arabia. It then coordinated the flow of information and assistance to opposition groups fighting on the southern front in Syria. MOC, in effect, unified the operations of those groups not only on a tactical level, but on a strategic one as well. Opposition groups throughout Syria began copying MOC by setting up their own operations rooms. This enabled them not only to achieve a brief tactical coordination, it made it possible for them to wage major campaigns that spun out over time.

By autumn 2015, the Syrian army was reeling. The opposition had pushed it back to a defensive line that was steadily shrinking.

Then the reversal was itself reversed.

In July 2015, Bashar al-Assad made a formal request to Russian president Vladimir Putin, asking for direct Russian intervention to fight "jihadi terror" in Syria. The Russians deployed warplanes, tanks, artillery, cruise missiles, and paramilitary forces to reinforce the depleted Syrian military. Russian airpower, targeting both military and civilian targets, was crucial to the Syrian government's victory in the Battle of Aleppo. The regime and its allies managed to wrest control of Syria's largest city from opposition forces. The Russian air campaign was both vicious and indiscriminate: it damaged more than 33,000 residential buildings, targeted hospitals, and killed more than four hundred civilians, including ninety children. The battle proved to be the turning point in the conflict. The Syrian army and supporting militias regained both the initiative and territory, particularly in the north and along the vital Damascus-Aleppo highway.

Once again, foreign intervention had changed the course of the Syrian civil war. The opposition was never again able to gain the initiative.

### How did the conflict in Libya begin?

In Libya, a coalition of groups issued a call on social media for Libyans to participate in a Day of Rage to protest political and economic conditions. The date they chose was February 17, 2011. Events overtook the Day of Rage, however. On February 15, the Libyan government arrested Fathi Terbil, a lawyer who represented the families of inmates of Abu Salim prison whom the regime murdered during a prison riot in 1996. The inmates, many of whom belonged to the Islamist opposition to Qaddafi, demanded better living conditions and the return of privileges that had been revoked. To press their demands, they took hostages. In response, guards herded inmates into courtyards where they threw grenades and opened gunfire, killing about twelve hundred.

Soon after Terbil's arrest, several hundred family members and their supporters gathered at the headquarters of a local Revolutionary Committee, an arm of the regime, in Benghazi. They clashed with security forces. By the time the actual Day of Rage rolled around, six thousand protesters were in the streets of Benghazi calling for the overthrow of the regime, and protests and clashes had already spread to a number of towns surrounding Libya's second-largest city, which protesters declared to be "liberated" from the regime.

It is not surprising that the uprising broke out in eastern Libya, where government control was less concentrated than in the west. It was there that resentments about higher unemployment and lower government investment festered. But within days the uprising had spread to Libya's capital, Tripoli, where protesters set fire to government buildings and engaged government forces in street battles. It soon spread to other cities and towns as far west as the Tunisian border.

### What's behind the chaos in Libya?

From the beginning, the Libyan regime met the uprising that had broken out in Benghazi with an appalling level of violence. Security forces and the military treated the protesters as combatants. Government forces forswore teargas for live fire, and the government deployed helicopter gunships to put down the uprising in Tripoli. Elite units under the command of four of Qaddafi's seven sons remained loyal, of course. So did the twenty-five-hundred-man Islamic Pan-African Brigade, made up of fighters from Chad, Sudan, and Niger. Most of the air force, whose leaders were affiliated with Qaddafi's tribe, and the security forces, which consisted of members of Qaddafi's family and tribe and members of allied tribes, also remained loyal. Qaddafi had lavished his special units with military hardware while starving the regular army of resources to prevent a coup.

Regime violence in Libya, like regime violence in Syria, catalyzed a violent response. In Libya this took the form of local and tribal-based militias, as well as Islamist ones. Defectors from the military fought in or alongside various militias. Initially, the militias were no match for the units of the Libyan military loyal to the regime. Then, as government forces pushed eastward toward Benghazi, the United Nations Security Council passed Resolution 1973. The resolution authorized member states "acting nationally or through regional organizations . . . to take all necessary measures . . . to protect civilians and civilian populated areas under threat of attack."[3] Two of the three sponsors of the resolution were NATO members, and NATO's European members feared the loss of Libyan oil and a wave of immigration from Libya and sub-Saharan Africa should violence and anarchy continue. The alliance thus undertook an air campaign that pounded regime forces. The air campaign turned the tide of battle.

What should have been a postwar period of transition away from the authoritarian rule of Qaddafi and his clique toward something more benign began with promise. A National Transitional Council, made up of a diverse group of Libyans representing liberated cities and towns, arranged for elections to a General National Congress (GNC). Elections were held in July 2012. A little over half the seats went to secular parties and independents. Nevertheless, an Islamist bloc, led by a party affiliated with Libya's Muslim Brotherhood, forged a strategic alliance with independents, enabling it to set the agenda. That's when things began to fall apart.

Over time, Libyans grew increasingly disenchanted with legislative bickering and the increasing audacity of Islamist politicians and fighters. They also grew disenchanted with the political violence, which included the murder of the American ambassador by an Islamist militia in Benghazi. Participation in elections fell by two thirds from 2012 to 2014.

In 2014, Libyans went to the polls to elect a House of Representatives, which was to take over from the congress. Secular parties won overwhelmingly, but a number of Islamist members of the GNC refused to step aside or to dissolve the GNC, citing low voter turnout. They found support on the streets. Militias affiliated with the GNC seized control of Tripoli, forcing the newly elected members of the House of Representatives to flee to Tobruk in the east. There, they found support from forces under the control of General Khalifa Haftar, who had served under Qaddafi (and had once been a CIA asset). Haftar had been waging his own battle against select Islamist militias and political rivals in the east. In effect, the otherwise powerless House of Representatives provided the political cover for his ambitions.

Thus, beginning in 2014, Libya had two governments, both of which depended on force of arms for survival.

Then there were three.

In December 2015, the United Nations brokered an agreement between the rump GNC and the Tobruk government setting up a Government of National Accord (GNA). Although both sides soon renounced the agreement and refused to recognize the new government's authority, it remains the internationally recognized government of Libya. In April 2016, the GNC formally announced it was ceasing operations and, under pressure from militias associated with the GNA, withdrew from Tripoli. Three governments had once again become two.

In the meantime, the bloodshed continued, spurred on in large measure by outside powers. Some powers have supported the internationally recognized government, while others have supported Haftar's Libyan National Army (LNA). Among the former are Turkey and Qatar and, to a lesser extent, Italy. Among the latter are Saudi Arabia, the UAE, Egypt, Russia, and France. For all, the promise of a post-conflict payoff, be it access to oil, oilfield contracts, or exploitation of Libya's access to the Mediterranean, proved too alluring to forswear. As in Syria, foreign assistance has been both direct and indirect. Turkey deployed troops to Tripoli that saved the GNA from an assault by Haftar's forces. Russian mercenaries from the Wagner Group, better known for their role in the invasion of Ukraine, have fought on the other side, thanks to the generosity of the UAE, which picked up the tab. The UAE also bought arms and matériel for Haftar's forces, and hired mercenaries from Chad and Sudan to fight alongside them. Not to be outdone, Qatar has financed some of the largest militias fighting for the GNA.

As had taken place in Syria, foreign intervention, both direct and indirect, served to prolong and intensify Libya's agony.

### What is the conflict in Yemen about?

The Yemen conflict might be traced to the collision of two events: the 2011 uprising against the regime of Ali Abdullah Saleh—a local expression of the uprisings that swept the Arab

world from December 2010 to March 2011—and a separate rebellion that had begun in the northwest of the country in 2003.

The 2011 uprising in Yemen began much as the uprising in
Egypt had begun: with a protest movement led by students,
youth activists, and others, who demanded the immediate resignation of Saleh. They encamped outside Sana University in
Yemen's capital, just as Egyptian activists had done in Tahrir
Square. Planned protests began simultaneously elsewhere as
well and spread under their own momentum.

The regime in Yemen depended on the compliance, or at
least the quiescence, of influential tribal, political, and military leaders. It bought off those leaders and balanced them off
against one another. As the protest movement broadened its
base of support and spread throughout the country, and as the
regime's resort to ever-increasing levels of violence provoked
further resistance, those leaders smelled blood in the water
and began to defect. This, of course, increased the level of violence and expanded its breadth.

To end the violence, the Gulf Cooperation Council (GCC),
a Saudi-dominated association of Gulf monarchies, brokered
a deal, with the backing of the United States and the United
Nations. Saleh would step down as president and receive im-
munity, his vice president Abdu Rabbu Mansour Hadi would
assume the post of acting president, and Yemen's fate would
be placed in the hands of a National Dialogue Conference.
Hadi later ran unopposed for the post of president. He won
handily.

In theory, the conference was to bring together all the
stakeholders in Yemeni political life—from established
politicians to the youths who had taken to the streets to
women and civil society groups. In reality, it was dominated
by the usual suspects. The largest blocs of seats went to the
former ruling party and the parties of the loyal opposition
in the Yemeni parliament. They were more focused on the
reallocation of power among themselves than on reform.
Some stakeholders were not represented or complained of

underrepresentation or double-dealing. Among the latter were members of Ansar Allah (Partisans of Allah), who were allotted thirty-five seats out of a total of 565. They also objected to the terms of the federal scheme worked out by the conference and what they claimed was their relative disempowerment in that scheme.

The Ansar Allah is better known as "the Houthis," a name that refers to the most prominent clan within Yemen's Zaydi community. Zaydis practice a form of Shiʿi Islam, which differs from the strain of Shiʿism practiced in Iran and much of the rest of the Islamic world. They are thus a minority of a minority— although they make up approximately 40 percent of the population of Yemen, a sizable minority there.

The Houthis had waged an on again, off again, rebellion against the government of Ali Abdullah Saleh since 2004. Their grievances included the underdevelopment of northwest Yemen, where they were concentrated, and the heavy-handedness of the regime. They also resented the marginalization of Zaydis by the central government, which even sent out salafi clerics as missionaries to the region. Lest anyone be tempted to view the conflict in Yemen in religious terms, however, it should be noted that Ali Abdullah Saleh was also a Zaydi. At various points in the post-2011 conflict, he battled against the Houthis or in alliance with them, depending on the circumstances.

Circumstances for collusion were ripe in 2014, when the Houthis, on the one hand, and Saleh and his loyalists, on the other, joined forces against Saleh's former subordinate. They marched on Sana, taking the city in January 2015. They then turned their attention south and east toward Aden and the Red Sea coast. This proved too much for Saudi Arabia and the UAE. Both feared for the future of the compliant Hadi, whom the Houthis had deposed. They also feared that the Houthis would block their access to the vital Bab al-Mandeb waterway, which led to the Red Sea and the Suez Canal. They intervened, in the process sucking the United States and the United Kingdom into the quagmire. The two Western powers provided Saudi Arabia and the UAE with weapons, intelligence, and logistical support. The Gulf countries undertook a devastating air campaign, bombing civilian targets including hospitals and, in one case, a wedding party, killing twenty.

For their part, the Houthis reached out to Iran, which was responsive. While skeptical of the Houthi's unnecessarily provocative overreach, Iran is always willing to poke its adversaries in the eye.

Neither the Houthis nor the Gulf-supported government was capable of retaking all of Yemen. Nor was either capable of eliminating its rival. The conflict in Yemen thus settled into a stalemate.

### How has the intervention of outside powers prolonged civil conflict?

The first "street phase" of the Tunisian uprising—the period from the self-immolation of Muhammad Bouazizi to the flight of Zine al-Abidine bin Ali—lasted less than a month. The period between the occupation of Tahrir Square in Cairo and the resignation of Hosni Mubarak was even shorter. To be sure, the uprisings in Tunisia and Egypt lasted beyond their first acts, but the brevity and relative nonviolence of the mass mobilizations there does beg the question: Why was it that conflicts in Syria, Libya, and Yemen have lasted as long as they have—and with such violence?

In Tunisia and Egypt, the military decided that decapitating the regime was a better option than having it overthrown. This did not take place in Libya and Yemen. Both were weak states whose governments and militaries fragmented. This meant that there was no unified regime that might have sought accommodation with, or overpowered, its opponents. But Syria was hardly a weak state and the regime and its military arm held together.

Some observers have blamed the violence in Libya and Yemen on their "tribal character" and the reliance of governments there on tribal leaders to mediate between the government and the population. But, again, this theory doesn't account for events in Syria. Nor does it explain why a government's patronage of so-called tribal leaders should result in unremitting bloodshed any more than a government's patronage of any other type of power broker—say, trade union leaders or party bosses—would.

In short, there is no inherent reason why conflicts in the three states should prove to be intractable. Instead, we might find the reasons elsewhere. Foremost among these is the fact that conflicts became proxy wars in all three states.

Proxy wars are conflicts in which outside powers intervene either directly or indirectly on the side of a combatant or combatants. Those powers believe the victory of their clients or a continuation of the conflict would further their own strategic, economic, and/or political interests. Thus, the Russians and Iranians (along with Hizbullah) intervened (directly) in Syria to enhance the chances of the Syrian government to achieve victory; the United States intervened (indirectly) in Afghanistan during the 1980s to "bleed" the Soviet Union.

Proxy wars tend to be more violent and unrelenting than conflicts in which there is no outside interference. There is good reason for this. When out-and-out victory of one side or the other is impossible, only negotiations can bring about a settlement. Political scientists argue that negotiations among parties involved in a civil war—the most common sort of war since the end of the Period of Decolonization—can only succeed in ending hostilities when each side views a battlefield victory as impossible and continued warfare as injurious to itself as to its opponents. They call this a "mutually hurting stalemate."

If one side or the other thinks its goals can be achieved on the battlefield, however, there is little possibility of reaching a settlement. After all, why compromise if there is still the possibility of taking it all? Only after all sides in a civil war realize there is no possibility of achieving their goals through violence is the time ripe for negotiations (political scientists call this, cleverly, "ripeness theory"). They point to a number of examples of civil strife—in Northern Ireland, Bosnia, and elsewhere—that, they claim, prove this.

Foreign intervention into a civil war makes it difficult to achieve a mutually hurting stalemate and thus makes it difficult to achieve ripeness. Losing belligerents will naturally look to their foreign patrons to help them turn the tide. And those patrons are usually only too willing to help. Foreign backers of each side view the stakes not only in terms of a winning or losing proxy, but in the wider, more critical context that made them get involved in someone else's war in the first place. They are unlikely, therefore, simply to throw up their hands at the first signs of setback. Rather, under such circumstances they are more likely to ramp up their level of assistance to their proxies. When they do, their opponent is more likely to do the same, thus increasing the level of violence and further delaying the time of ripeness.

So, what have been the stakes for various outside powers in Syria, Libya, and Yemen? Saudi Arabia and Iran view the conflicts in Syria and Yemen in terms of a "zero sum game" pitting a state committed to the status quo (Saudi Arabia) against a state which views the post-uprisings period as one of opportunity to further its interests (Iran). A loss for one is a gain for the other, and vice versa. Russia, Turkey, the UAE, and Qatar seek to expand their influence and to realize great power pretensions (Russia), gain allies and access to natural gas fields below the Mediterranean (Turkey), dominate vital shipping lanes from the Arabian and Red Seas to the Mediterranean (UAE), and hedge its bets in a volatile region (Qatar). European powers are concerned about the effects of instability and unfriendly governments on immigration from North Africa, sub-Saharan Africa, and the Asiatic Middle East. They are also concerned about oil supplies and terrorism.

And, of course, there is the United States, whose only consistent goals since the administration of George W. Bush have been to extricate itself from commitments noteworthy for their diminishing returns, wage the endless Global War on Terrorism, and return to what might be called the *status quo ante*—without too much direct American involvement.

### How has warlordism affected conflicts in Syria, Libya, and Yemen?

The fact that conflicts in Syria, Libya, and Yemen became proxy wars is not the only reason they have been so bloody and protracted. Warlordism is also to blame.

The great German sociologist Max Weber once defined the state as the entity that holds the "monopoly of legitimate physical violence within a certain territory." What happens, however, when a central authority is absent or too weak to monopolize violence within a territory internationally recognized as a state? Power, then, might devolve to local political bosses or strongmen who are able to muster the resources that would enable them to operate autonomously. For warlords, those resources are twofold. First, they need the backing of militias or militia-type organizations that enable those warlords to fend off challengers within and without a given territory. They also need income derived from some form of rent—minerals, smuggling, extortion of populations under their sway— that enables them to maintain those militias or militia-type organizations.

Warlordism is more than the sum total of warlords and their entourages. Warlordism should be viewed as a system of political economy. Individual warlords may come and go, the size of the territories they control might get larger or smaller, the populations within those territories might increase or decrease. Nevertheless, the system as a whole is relatively stable because it is economically sustainable and can only be uprooted if a more powerful military force can impose its will.

And warlordism should not be seen as a "Middle Eastern thing." The quintessential examples of warlordism commonly cited by social scientists are China in the early twentieth century and medieval Europe, and a number of political scientists use contemporary Somalia as the starting point for their theorizing.

The last example is the one United Nations and Arab League envoy to Syria Lakhdar Brahimi drew from when discussing the probable endgame in Syria in December 2012: "What is going to happen is 'Somalization'—warlords and the Syrian people persecuted by people seizing its fate."[4]

Coming as it did before the regime's battlefield gains of 2015, Brahimi did not foresee the resilience of the Syrian government, enabled by foreign assistance. Yet that makes his Somalia analogy even more apt. It is probable that Syria, like Somalia, will have a single government, which would reign, but not rule, over the entirety of its territory. It is probable that it will have a permanent representative to the United Nations, issue passports and postage stamps, and even, if it so desired, send a team to the Olympics. However, as in the case of Somalia, it is also probable armed militias would control large swaths of territory outside the control of the government. There would be no established boundaries between the territories, which would engage in chest thumping and perpetual warfare against each other or sign on to informal truces. The world will inherit another failed state, this time in the heart of the Arab east.

The character of the insurgent forces gives credence to Brahimi's vision. Of the close to 150 groups listed in an October 2015 report published by the Institute for the Study of War, less than a third had a presence in more than one province and about half of those were located in only two. What this indicates is that over the course of the civil war, much of the indigenous opposition (along with indigenous militias supporting the government) came to consist of locally recruited fighters loyal to their neighborhood powerbroker.

His authority enabled him to wrest control of resources—oil, wheat, refineries, tolls from border crossings, protection money—from rival powerbrokers and the government. Together, the fighters and the powerbrokers inhabit a self-perpetuating war economy upon which they depend. As one observer has noted, "opposition-held Syria is Mad Max meets The Sopranos."[5] Unable to dismantle this system or overwhelm autonomous powerbrokers, the weakened government will likely have to learn to cope with them.

A similar fate might await Libya and Yemen. In Libya, militias associated with the GNA battle those associated with Haftar's LNA, when they are not battling each other. The LNA itself consists of approximately seven thousand core members and eighteen thousand auxiliary fighters grouped into Chadian, Sudanese, and tribal and "pick-up" militias. As in Syria, they find sustenance in an economy that is based upon the extraction of rent, the big prizes being control of Libya's oilfields, oil infrastructure, and oil exports, along with smuggling and human trafficking; Tripoli, its resources, and patronage networks; and "strategic rent"—that is, payments from foreign powers which expect the militias to act in their interests.

As for Yemen, a UN-appointed Panel of Experts issued a report in 2018 that began, "After nearly three years of conflict, Yemen, as a State, has all but ceased to exist. Instead of a single State there are warring statelets, and no one side has either the political support or the military strength to reunite the country or to achieve victory on the battlefield."[6] By the time the report was written, the Houthis had cemented their control over their traditional base in the country's northwest. Elsewhere in Yemen, a dizzying array of militias and political parties governed the territory claimed by the government.

In 2022, the Saudis and Emiratis, the two main sponsors of the militias, engineered the replacement of Hadi by a Presidential Leadership Council. The council included representatives of the largest groups. The creation of the council, made up of groups with widely divergent agendas (including an Emirati-backed faction whose goal is the creation of an independent southern Yemen) freezes the system of warlordism in place.

### What have been the consequences of conflict in Syria, Libya, and Yemen?

The repercussions of conflict in Syria, Libya, and Yemen have been horrific for populations living in those countries. The conflicts have also had significant effects elsewhere.

According to the Syrian Observatory for Human Rights, 494,438 Syrians died during the first decade of the civil war, including about 160,000 civilians. Of Syria's 22 million people, more than half have been forced to leave their homes. About 6.8 million ended up as refugees forced to shelter outside Syria and 6.9 million are internally displaced. Many can never return to the homes they had left because those homes no longer exist: during the first five years of the conflict alone, fighting destroyed about two million of 4.7 million homes. The Russian-dominated air campaign over Aleppo alone damaged or destroyed 35,000 structures in Syria's largest city. By the beginning of 2022, about 14.6 million Syrians needed some form of humanitarian assistance. About a third of them have been classified as being in "catastrophic need."

Statistics can, of course, convey only so much. Here is how one activist described Homs three years into the uprising:

Once a thriving city of approximately 700,000, [Homs] is today a broken ruin. The regime loyalist Alawi-majority districts are today the only areas of the city where normal life continues. Regime bombs have fallen relentlessly every day on the rest of the city, destroying apartment buildings, shops, and historic mosques. Entire districts, such as Khalidiya, Baba Amr, Jourat al Shiah, Bayada and

Warsha have been emptied of their inhabitants and completely destroyed. Many of Homs's residents have fled
from the centre of the city to the outer suburbs, such as
Wa'r, which has taken in at least 200,000 refugees and is
completely surrounded by the regime. Others are now
outside the city or outside the country. In the Old City,
not a single building remains intact and the siege on the
inhabitants was complete and total. . . . No food was
allowed to enter—starvation and deaths from treatable
injuries were the norm. Residents had to bring in their
food from under the sewers to avoid starvation.

"The Syrian revolution began with protests calling for freedom,
democracy, and dignity," he concludes, "but it could end with
a nightmare of sectarian cleansing and genocide."[7]

Syria, Libya, and Yemen all serve as nodal points in global
flow of refugees. Oddly, both Libya and Yemen host significant numbers of refugees and migrants, some fleeing conflicts
or poverty at home, others trapped while in transit elsewhere.
It is, however, the outflow of refugees from Syria that has had
outsized effects both regionally and globally. Most Syrian
refugees have fled to Turkey (3.6 million), Lebanon (831,000),
Jordan (675,000), Iraq (260,000), and Egypt (141,300). While
92 percent of refugees live outside refugee camps, unemployment is high and 70 percent live in poverty with another
15 percent facing poverty as a result of the post-pandemic economic downturn in the region. The international community
picks up some of the tab, but the burden for providing munic-
ipal services such as lighting and the delivery of clean water,
as well as healthcare and educational services, falls on the host
countries. Needless to say, this puts a strain on a host country's
economy, social fabric, and generosity.

And it is not a problem that will go away soon. Between
2017 and 2021 only 4 percent of Syrian refugees returned to
Syria. Most refugees cited safety as their biggest concern.

According to both the UNHCR and the European Union, Syria remains unsafe, making their voluntary ("spontaneous") return unlikely, while repatriation by force would be a violation of international law. Besides, the Syrian government does not want its potential opponents back. Xenophobic reaction in Europe and the United States has closed off those venues for resettlement as well. The possible influx of Syrian refugees fueled populist anti-immigrant sentiments in both places. In the United States, this took the form of the Trump administration's so-called Muslim ban.

Conditions in Libya and Yemen parallel those in Syria. Before the ousting of Qaddafi, Libyans enjoyed one of the highest standards of living in Africa. Libya does, after all, sit on Africa's largest pool of oil. The good times (if any times under Qaddafi might be considered good) were not to last. With the onset of the conflict, control of oilfields and the National Oil Company became a political football, and protests and militia activity effectively ended exports (exports resumed in July 2022). By the beginning of 2020, 900,000–1.3 million Libyans out of a population of 6.8 million were in need of humanitarian assistance. This included 200,000 internally displaced persons.

Conflict affected Libyans in another way as well: unexploded ordnance and land mines laid by Hafter's forces and the Wagner Group during the siege of Tripoli still litter close to 280 square miles south of the capital, where they inflict casualties and prevent residents from returning home. Land mines came to symbolize Libya's conflict much as barrel bombs did Syria's.

As the Arab world's poorest country, Yemen's pre-conflict profile was the polar opposite of Libya's. Nevertheless, the war added to Yemenis' misery by bringing a disruption in trade and a Saudi blockade of Yemen's seaports and border crossings. This, in turn, led to famine and the spread of disease among a malnourished population that depends on imports for 97 percent of its grain supply. As of 2022, more than sixteen million out of a population of about thirty million required emergency food assistance (a problem exacerbated by the war in Ukraine, a major grain supplier to Yemen), and eighteen million were without clean water and sanitation. Included among them were 4.3 million internally displaced persons, many of whom lived in what are euphemistically called "informal displacement sites" where cholera, diphtheria, measles, and Dengue Fever run rampant. Of the 370,000 Yemenis who have died as a result of the conflict, the United Nations Development Programme estimates that 60 percent died from war induced shortages of food, water, and health services.

Conflict in Syria, Libya, and Yemen has not only triggered a humanitarian nightmare, it has led to the emergence of ungoverned internal frontiers in those states—spaces in which jihadist groups such as al-Qaeda and ISIS might cluster. While the al-Qaeda affiliate, al-Qaeda in the Arabian Peninsula (AQAP), has found sanctuary in the badlands of Yemen, ISIS affiliates dominate the jihadist world in Syria and Libya.

### Has Syria become a narco-state?

In September 2022, the Qatar-based news network *al-Jazeera* posted an article with the bizarre title, "Syria Seizes Hummus Bowls Made out of Crushed Captagon Pills."[8] The article goes on to explain that Syrian authorities had arrested an individual who had crushed and reconstituted (in the form of pottery) more than fifty pounds of the amphetamine. Obviously, someone had ticked off the wrong authorities or failed to pay off the right ones.

Just as America has its fentanyl/opioid crisis, the Middle East—particularly Jordan and the GCC states—has its Captagon crisis. For Syria, Captagon is a multi-billion-dollar-a-year business. In 2020 alone, Syria exported an estimated $16 billion worth of Captagon. As a matter of fact, Captagon is by far the most lucrative Syrian export. It certainly has proved more lucrative than Syria's other export commodities, which currently include olive oil and copper and copper alloys, presumably looted from factories and private houses and sold, mostly, in Egypt. Those commodities provide only a tiny fraction of Syria's export income.

Captagon manufacture and export began as a byproduct of Syria's warlord-dominated economy. The drug was introduced mainly by opposition militias in territory ceded by the government in the early stages of the conflict, when much of Syria resembled the Wild West. Soon pro-government and Kurdish militias entered the market, attracted by high profits, large swaths of unpoliced territory and anarchic cities, and porous frontiers manned by corrupt and corruptible border guards. When the government began to retake territory previously held by opposition forces, it, too, got into the act. Since 2018, the Syrian government has dominated the trade in illicit Captagon, enriching entities and authorities who oversee the production of the drug on an industrial scale.

And not just any authorities, either. Members of Bashar al-Assad's inner circle have discovered the easy profits they (and the Syrian state) might reap from narco-trafficking. Among them are Maher al-Assad, the president's brother and commander of the Fourth Armored Division, Wasim Badia al-Assad, the president's cousin and militia leader, and Samer al-Assad, another cousin who oversees Captagon production in the Alawite-dominated port city of Latakia. Elements of the military and local and foreign militias provide shipping, supply, muscle, and access to ports and border crossings. Unbeknownst to the wealthy young addicts who first try the drug on a lark, they are financing the Syrian government's war machine.

Power in Syria is no longer just in the hands of politicians and their cronies; it is in the hands of a drug cartel.

### What is ISIS?

The Islamic State of Iraq and Syria (ISIS) is a group committed to salafi principles and jihadi tactics. Its origins might be traced to two sources: al-Qaeda's renegade affiliate in Iraq and the

American invasion of Iraq. Abu Musab al-Zarqawi, a Jordanian-born gangbanger, established al-Qaeda in Mesopotamia after meeting with Osama bin Laden in Afghanistan. Bin Laden harbored doubts about al-Zarqawi. It was not that bin Laden doubted al-Zarqawi's commitment to waging jihad against the United States after it invaded Iraq in 2003. It was that he disapproved of al-Zarqawi's commitment to waging jihad against Iraqi Shi'is, whom al-Zarqawi considered apostates from true Islam. Nevertheless, he gave al-Zarqawi a seed grant to establish his own al-Qaeda franchise.

After al-Zarqawi's death in an American airstrike in 2006, his organization went through several permutations. Then Abu Bakr al-Baghdadi, who received religious training in Baghdad and had been imprisoned by the American occupation forces, took over and rechristened it the "Islamic State of Iraq." After Syrian-born fighters in his group asked to be allowed to return home to fight there, he again changed the name, this time to the Islamic State of Iraq and Syria. While observers have frequently attributed its military successes to its ultra-violence and ideology, the former Iraqi military officers who had served under Saddam Hussein and who played an important role in ISIS's military campaigns deserve most of the credit. They were at the forefront of the campaign that swatted away a reconstructed Iraqi army enfeebled by corruption, sectarianism, and political patronage.

ISIS is noted for its brutality. The group has regularly beheaded and crucified those it considers its enemies, killed other Muslims for the crime of apostasy (leaving the fold), and has committed acts of genocide against those it considers polytheists. It has sponsored terrorist outrages abroad. In summer 2014, it conquered a broad swath of territory stretching from north/central Syria through central Iraq. The territory included the third-largest city in Iraq, Mosul. A year later, it began a global campaign of terrorist attacks.

Salafi/jihadi groups like ISIS adhere to much the same ideology. They all want to reconstruct their societies along the lines of what they believe to be proper Islamic principles. They do, however, differ in strategy. Many focus on overthrowing homegrown dictators and replacing them with regimes committed to enforcing a rigid interpretation of Islam. Al-Qaeda, on the other hand, focuses on what it calls the "far enemy"—the Crusader-Zionist conspiracy that includes not only the United States and Israel but all those it perceives to be the enemies of Islam. Its strategy is to "vex and exhaust" its enemies by drawing them into far-flung adventures, like the Soviets, then the Americans, in Afghanistan. The American invasion and occupation of Iraq played right into its hands.

ISIS is unique because it has territorial ambitions. Its strategy has been to seize territory and purify it from foreign influences and from those it considers "unIslamic"—Yazidis, secular Kurds, Shiʿis, etc. Overall, its strategy can be reduced to three words: *khilafa*, *takfir*, and *hijra*.

*Khilafa* means "caliphate"—the form of governance under which most Muslims lived after the death of Muhammad. Al-Baghdadi believes that Islam requires a caliphate—governance that is in accordance with Islamic law over territory. That territory should be under the authority of a caliph—that is, a righteous and knowledgeable descendant of the prophet. When his forces took over Mosul in the summer of 2014, al-Baghdadi proclaimed himself caliph and renamed the "Islamic State of Iraq and Syria" the "Islamic State."

*Takfir* is the act of pronouncing Muslims who disagree with ISIS's strict interpretation of Islamic law to be apostates, a crime punishable by death. This is the reason for ISIS's murderous rampages against Shiʿis. While al-Qaeda central found these rampages counterproductive (the real enemy was the Americans, after all), ISIS leaders found them strategically beneficial. They believed they would provoke tit-for-tat Sunni-Shiʿi killings that would mobilize the Sunni community against the invaders. ISIS's ideology might be branded a form of Sunni nationalism.

The final word is *hijra*, the migration of Muslims from *dar al-harb* (the abode of war; i.e., non-Muslim majority countries) to *dar al-Islam* (the abode of Islam). The model for this is Muhammad and his early companions, who migrated from Mecca to Medina, where they established the first permanent Islamic community. ISIS leaders wanted a great incoming of Muslims into the caliphate. Not only did they wish to attract skilled administrators and fighters, they considered emigration from "non-Muslim territory" to "Muslim territory" a religious obligation. By 2015, the caliphate had attracted to its territory upward of 30,000 fighters. These came not only from the Middle East (outside of Iraq and Syria, the largest numbers came from Saudi Arabia and Tunisia), but also from North America, Europe, and elsewhere. According to a number of analysts, most were probably attracted by ISIS's ultra-violent reputation and ganglike ethos, not religious duty. ISIS was never able to attract skilled administrators and technicians in sufficient numbers, undercutting its capacity for state-building.

At its height, the ISIS caliphate governed a territory in Iraq and Syria the size of the United Kingdom and ruled over eight million people. ISIS's caliphate looked and functioned like a normal state—a particularly vicious one, it is true, but a state nonetheless. It issued license plates and building permits, had a courts and educational system, and attempted (but ultimately failed) to issue its own currency. It even had a flag and a national anthem. ISIS financed all this from a one-time infusion of cash from banks it looted during its conquests and from other sources. These ranged from the sale of oil and ancient artifacts and ransoms from kidnapped locals and foreigners, to alms, taxes, and other forms of extortion and confiscation. In other words, ISIS's method of finance resembled that of any other warlord.

ISIS ran its caliphate according to its interpretation of Islamic law, which, for ISIS, covers all aspects of people's lives, public and private (according to ISIS, the two separate domains don't exist in Islam). Its purview ran the gamut from diet and gender relations to mandatory prayers and charity. It prohibited alcohol and public smoking. According to the ISIS legal code, the penalty for drinking and smoking was eighty lashes, although repeat offenders faced execution. It strictly regulated dress. Women had to cover themselves; men, wear beards. Only married couples or immediate family members could mix with members of the opposite sex in public. Makeup for girls was prohibited, as were jeans. The penalty for engaging in homosexual acts was death; those caught were commonly thrown off buildings. Shops had to close during prayers. And citizens of the caliphate had to sing its national anthem a capella, because ISIS believed the use of musical instruments violated Islamic law.

### What legacy did the ISIS caliphate leave the Middle East and the world?

In August 2014, the United States began an air campaign against the ISIS caliphate, which, by that time, controlled about a third of Syria and 40 percent of Iraq. A month later, the US expanded its operations to Syria. Within four and a half years, the American-led coalition had dislodged ISIS from all the territory it had conquered save a small number of villages on the Syrian-Iraqi border. Key to this victory were Kurdish militias on the ground in both Iraq and Syria. They exacted revenge against ISIS for the outrages the group inflicted on Yazidi Kurds.

The administration of Barack Obama cited a number of reasons for its intervention, from ISIS-sponsored terrorism to humanitarian concerns. In an interview in the *Atlantic*, however, Obama inadvertently showed his hand about what might have been the true, underlying reason. Citing the 2008 Batman movie *The Dark Knight*, the former president explained,

There's a scene in the beginning in which the gang leaders of Gotham are meeting. . . .These are men who had the city divided up. They were thugs, but there was a kind of order. Everyone had his turf. And then the Joker comes in and lights the whole city on fire. ISIL [the Islamic State of Iraq and the Levant, Obama's term for ISIS] is the Joker. It has the capacity to set the whole region on fire. That's why we have to fight it.[9]

In other words, by uniting Syria and Iraq in a caliphate, and by threatening their neighbors, ISIS was on the verge of redrawing the map of the region. The United States intervened to preserve the state system there.

While the destruction of the ISIS caliphate preserved the state system in the region, ISIS fighters and affiliates have soldiered on. And even though the caliphate no longer exists, the legacy of ISIS continues.

Even before ISIS reached the limits of its expansion in Syria and Iraq, it had cast its eye elsewhere, where it has weakened and destabilized states. ISIS affiliates thrive in places that lack effective governance. One of the largest and most successful was established in Libya. Taking advantage of the anarchic conditions there, it took control over the coastal city of Sirte and the surrounding area. It also established a presence in Benghazi, before Haftar's forces drove it out. In the Sinai Peninsula of Egypt, ISIS has recruited from among disaffected and impoverished bedouin, al-Qaeda renegades, and Egyptian veterans of wars in Iraq and Afghanistan. ISIS's Sinai branch became an intractable and debilitating thorn in the side of a regime whose reason for being was its promise to restore stability. Other affiliates sprang up or were implanted by ISIS in Algeria, Saudi Arabia, Yemen, the Caucasus, Afghanistan/Pakistan (where it battles al-Qaeda), the Philippines, and Nigeria. The Nigerian affiliate came about when Boko Haram—a salafi/

jihadi group responsible for about 20,000 deaths in West Africa—pledged allegiance to ISIS and defected en masse.

ISIS has decimated ancient minority communities. As part of the process of conquest, ISIS sought to "purify" the territory it was taking over. This meant putting to flight or killing "apostates" such as Shi'is and secular Kurds and "polytheists" such as Yazidis. When ISIS took over Mosul, thirty thousand Mosuli Christians fled. ISIS was particularly brutal to the Yazidis, however. During its conquest of Sinjar in northwest Iraq, ISIS fighters slaughtered between two thousand and five thousand Yazidi men, sold more than three thousand Yazidi women and girls into slavery, and drove about fifty thousand Yazidis into the mountains where they faced starvation and dehydration.

Along with the decimation of minority communities, ISIS inflicted incalculable damage on the cultural heritage of the areas it occupied. ISIS purposefully vandalized or destroyed some of the richest archaeological sites in the world. ISIS destroyed monuments, statuary, and the remains of ancient buildings in such storied ancient habitats as Palmyra, Apamea, and Dura-Europos in Syria and Ninevah and Nimrod in Iraq. For ISIS, ancient relics represent idolatry and violate what it claims to be Islamic prohibitions against representational art. Looting ancient sites also provided ISIS an important source of revenue, and their destruction displayed ISIS's power for destruction and defiance to the world and would-be recruits.

Finally, ISIS has been responsible for terrorist attacks globally. ISIS had called on supporters early on to attack military and police targets where those supporters lived, but the wave of ISIS terrorism in Europe and the United States expanded dramatically after fall 2015. That was when coalition forces had begun to roll back the caliphate and, it seems, ISIS leadership sought to open up another front against its enemies. At the end of October of that year, ISIS's Sinai affiliate claimed credit for setting off a bomb on a Russian airliner, killing 224 passengers. Two weeks later, terrorists associated with ISIS launched a series of attacks in Paris, including one at the Bataclan Theater which killed 89 concertgoers. Overall, from 2013 to 2016—the height of the terror campaign—the Global Terrorism Database recorded 5,676 attacks attributed to ISIS members or hangers-on. Most were carried out by so-called lone wolves (although the RAND Corporation prefers the term "flaming bananas" to avoid glamorizing them[10]). And while a vast majority of the attacks took place in the Middle East, no region of the world was spared.

### What is Rojava?

In Kurdish, Rojava means "the land where the sun sets"—that is, western Kurdistan. It comprises a swath of territory in northern and eastern Syria that Kurdish-led forces liberated from ISIS and direct Syrian government control. (In 2018, it adopted the name "Autonomous Administration of North and East Syria," but is still commonly known by its original, shorter, and far more romantic moniker.) It is, for the time being, the site of a radical experiment in self-government that is unprecedented in the Middle East and, perhaps, anywhere.

The key to understanding the Rojava project (as those involved often refer to it) is the notion of "confederalism" as outlined in the "Federal Democratic Rojava Social Contract," the constitution of the territory. The contract was first proposed in January 2014, then ratified at the end of 2016. Confederalism refers to a system of governance in which local units (in this case, "autonomous regions") come together in a federation yet retain a great deal of autonomy. The constitution is so serious about devolving power to the regions that it stipulates that each region (there are three of them, along with seven sub-regions) has its own flag. And within each region, local elected councils are in charge. Confederalism in Rojava thus represents a governmental structure that is the direct opposite of the top-down, centralized structure of states in the region.

Rojava differs in other ways as well. Its charter guarantees freedom of expression and assembly and equality of all religious communities and languages. It mandates direct democracy and gender equality. Men and women share every position at every level of governance. It imposes term limits for politicians. It defines the state as secular and forbids the participation of religious leaders in politics. It even affirms the right of all citizens to a healthy environment.

Surrounding states also have constitutions with eloquent endorsements of political and human rights, so what's new? The difference with Rojava is that the constitutionally mandated structure of government and guarantee of rights is up and running. The common fight against ISIS, the role women played in that fight as members of the all-female Women's Protective Unit militia, and the trauma ISIS brought to the territory reinforced egalitarian bonds and democratic practices within Rojava.

There are, however, aspects of the Rojava project that give some observers pause. There is the perpetual jockeying for position among rival Kurdish clans and the struggle for preeminence among Turkish, Syrian, and Iraqi Kurds that threatened the project from the beginning. There is the continuing troubled relationship between Kurds, on the one hand, and Arabs and other groups, on the other. This began in the 1960s when the Syrian government began moving other populations to the territory to challenge Kurdish dominance there. And in the aftermath of the war against ISIS, it became routine for the predominantly Kurdish Syrian Democratic Forces—the militia fighting ISIS—to presume that the residents of villages that ISIS had occupied, along with non-Kurdish refugees from ISIS-held territory, to have collaborated with ISIS and treat them accordingly.

Then there are the problematic origins of Rojava. The Syrian-Kurdish Democratic Union Party (PYD) played an outsized role in the project. The PYD is affiliated with the leftist Kurdistan Workers' Party (PKK), a group that has fought against the Turkish government, first for the independence of Kurds in Turkey, then for their autonomy there. Both Turkey and the United States have designated the PKK a terrorist organization. Much of the population of Rojava looks to Abdullah Ocalan (pronounced OH-ja-lahn), the founder of the PKK, with cult-like devotion. It was Ocalan's enthusiasm for confederalism that encouraged Syrian Kurds to adopt it in the first place.

The association of Rojava with the PKK and Ocalan is the reason Turkey launched its incursion into northern Syria in 2018. When Donald Trump announced the withdrawal of American troops from northern Syria, the Turks invaded again. American forces had not only been allied with the Syrian Kurds in the fight against ISIS—a fight in which the Syrian Kurds had fought and died disproportionately—their presence in Rojava acted as a tripwire that prevented the Turks from attacking again. Their withdrawal put the Rojava project in harm's way.

The Turks claim that their goal is to establish a buffer zone along Turkey's southern border and move one million of the 3.7 million Syrian refugees in Turkey there. Their incursion would thus kill two birds with one stone. Complicating matters, however, is the renewed presence of the Syrian army in Rojava. When the Turks began their assault, the Kurds put their lives in the hands of the Syrian government, which vowed that it would protect them. However, the Syrian government will never countenance Kurdish autonomy in Syria. The reason for this is that Rojava sits atop the largest oilfields in Syria and the Syrian government wants them back. The fact that Syrian Kurds found themselves caught between their Turkish enemy and their Syrian government "friend" dooms the Rojava project.

Nevertheless, for all its flaws, the Rojava project actualized the democratic impulses of the Arab uprisings of 2010-2011. It not only showed what is possible, it offers an off-the-shelf blueprint available for future use.

## What's behind the meltdown of Lebanon?

On August 4, 2020, an errant spark from a welder's torch ignited fireworks stored in Warehouse 12 at the Port of Beirut. The fireworks detonated 2,750 tons of ammonium nitrate—the same explosive used in the Oklahoma City bombing of 1995. The compound had been stored at the port since 2013. The blast—loud enough to be heard in Cyprus—ripped through the port, then adjoining neighborhoods of the city. It killed more than 200, injured about 7,000, displaced more than 300,000, and caused more than $4.6 billion in damages.

Much about the blast remains a mystery. Why had highly explosive ammonium nitrate, off-loaded from a damaged ship, been allowed to fester in a warehouse at the port for seven years? What did the four governments and three prime ministers between 2013 and 2020 know about it? Were there really 2,750 tons of the substance in storage, or had gangs associated with various Lebanese political factions siphoned off an unknown quantity to redistribute or sell? Was the explosion really touched off by an errant spark, or was there something more sinister afoot? These questions linger because political elites who control Lebanese politics have stymied an official investigation. They not only fear that such an investigation would find fault with one or more of their number, they fear that its conclusions would undercut the very system from which they derive their power. Little wonder, then, that the explosion came to symbolize systemic corruption and incompetence of political elites for a broad swath of the Lebanese public who already had had enough.

The constitution of Lebanon guarantees representation for all eighteen officially recognized religious sects in the government and civil service, although the president, prime minister, and speaker of parliament must be, respectively, a Maronite Christian, a Sunni Muslim, and a Shiʻi Muslim. From time to time, the leaders of each community—think of them as political bosses—haggle with the leaders of other communities about their share of the "take." They draw up electoral lists, fill positions in cabinets and the bureaucracy, and oversee the distribution of patronage—a school here, a soup kitchen there—to their communities. This is what makes Lebanon a sectarian oligarchy. It is in their interest to keep national institutions weak, the better to safeguard their power and revenue stream. As Ray Liotta's character put it in the movie *Goodfellas*, "It's like a license to steal. It's a license to do anything." And it seemed to work for everyone's benefit—until the cupboard was bare.

After the end of the 1975-1990 civil war (which ended up tweaking Lebanon's post-independence political system rather than overhauling it), the Lebanese economy depended on remittances and the infusion of cash from the vast Lebanese diaspora, foreign aid, tourism, and, most important, borrowing from abroad and domestically. And in the second decade of the twenty-first century, the central bank came to rely on borrowing from Lebanon's commercial banks at exorbitant interest rates to finance government spending (it should come as no surprise that relatives of prominent politicians controlled many of those banks). Servicing the debt, along with the usual payoffs associated with patronage politics—like jobs in a bloated public sector—meant that there was little left over to pay for essential needs, such as infrastructure. This is why one-third of Lebanese acquired their electricity from private generators and not from the dysfunctional national grid.

Then came a number of shocks. These included the Syrian civil war and the influx of refugees, a decline in foreign infusions of cash (a result of donor fatigue and US sanctions meant to target Hizbullah and its patron, Iran), COVID-19 and COVID-19-induced lockdowns, and the Ukraine war. In 2019, banks declared a holiday and closed their doors, leaving their depositors high and dry. The Lebanese pound lost 90 percent of its value. By mid-2021 inflation had reached 281 percent. Almost 80 percent of the Lebanese population was reduced to poverty. According to the World Bank, the collapse of the

Lebanese economy was one of the three greatest economic disasters in the past 150 years.

Lebanese have reacted in a number of ways. Some have opted out—literally. Almost eighty thousand Lebanese emigrated in 2020, an increase of 346 percent from the previous year. Others have taken to the streets.

Beginning October 2019, Lebanese participated in multiple protests throughout the country. Triggered by the announcement by the government of a raft of new taxes, including one on the free messaging app Whatsapp, underlying the protests was anger at multiple government failures. Among those failures was the inability of firefighters to extinguish devastating wildfires near Beirut because the government had not allocated money for the maintenance of their equipment. But protesters did not target government ineptitude alone: they challenged the sectarian system itself. By 2022, polls indicated 90 percent of Lebanese opposed it. Hence, the popular protest slogan *Killon ya'ni killon* (all means all)—meaning all the political bosses had to go.

That is not likely to happen soon. Unable to reach a power-sharing agreement and unwilling to stand down, those bosses proved resilient. They also proved unwilling to take any steps that might diminish their power or strengthen their political rivals. In the meantime, the IMF all but walked away from its offer of a $3 billion bailout (with strings attached) to mitigate disaster.

At the end of July 2022, a block of enormous grain silos, partly damaged by the 2020 explosion at the Port of Beirut, caught fire in the summer heat and collapsed. Each silo stored 2,500 tons of grain. The collapse occurred as protesters gathered to mark the second anniversary of the port disaster.

### How fragile is the regime in Iran?

On September 13, 2022, members of Iran's "Guidance Patrol"—commonly known as the "morality police"—took twenty-two-year-old Mahsa (Zhina) Amini into custody at a Tehran metro station. They accused Amini of not wearing her headscarf—her hijab—correctly. She died in custody three days later. Authorities said her death was caused by a heart condition, although she had no history of heart problems. Her father claimed that he had seen bruises on her legs, making the case for foul play even more compelling.

Events then unfolded much as they had in Tunisia after the self-immolation of Muhammad Bouazizi and in Syria after the arrest of the graffiti-writing children. Protests broke out in Amini's hometown of Saqez, in Iranian Kurdistan (Amini was Kurdish Iranian). They then spread to Sanandaj, the regional capital. Protesters there shouted "Death to the dictator" (meaning Ayatollah Ali Khameini, Iran's Supreme Guide), and women removed their own hijabs in defiance of regime prescription. The government responded with violence, going so far as ordering the use of live ammunition and the execution of arrested activists. Hospital workers noted the unusually high number of women with gunshot wounds to their faces, breasts, and genitals. The government also organized counter-demonstrations of its own.

Protests continued to spread, and women continued publicly to unveil. Within weeks, protesters had taken to the streets in close to two hundred cities and towns across Iran. Among them were the shrine cities of Qom and Mashhad, where future ayatollahs—high-ranking Shi'i clerics—receive their training. Shopkeepers in Tehran closed their doors for a three-day general strike, and oilfield workers walked off the job. In all, by the end of 2022, there had been 225 union and 344 non-union strikes in conjunction with the protests. The regime faced its worst domestic crisis since the establishment of the Islamic Republic in 1979.

This was not the first time Iranians had taken to the streets since the 1979 revolution. In 2009, there were mass protests— the "Green Revolution"—decrying the results of a presidential election many Iranians viewed as fraudulent (in some cities, there were more voters than residents). Protests over economic mismanagement and fuel price increases broke out in 2017 and 2019. But the 2022–2023 protests were different in a fundamental way. While women had participated alongside men in earlier protests, in the more recent round they catalyzed the rebellion and played a starring role.

After years of a more relaxed enforcement of compulsory dress codes for women, a hard-line president, Ebrahim Raisi, replaced his reformist predecessor in 2021 and beefed up enforcement of dress code regulations. The anger sparked by Amini's death and government-enforced misogyny might be seen in the rituals and slogans of protesters. During protests, women not only removed their hijabs, they sometimes burned them, and they cut their hair in a symbolic gesture of outrage and mourning. While they did so, protesters chanted "Woman, life, freedom"—which became as ubiquitous in the Iranian protests as "The people want the fall of the regime" had become in the uprising in Egypt. The slogan was first chanted at Amini's funeral.

Women are second-class citizens in the Islamic Republic. While they make up half of all college students, women's workforce participation was 14 percent in 2020. Employment discrimination against women is widespread, and those with jobs can expect to make 18 percent of what their male colleagues make. Child marriage is on the rise (girls as young as thirteen can legally be married). Husbands can make decisions for their wives, including what jobs they can get and whether they can get passports and travel abroad. And women are not allowed to sing in public or ride bicycles. It is telling that Saudi and Iranian officials have used the treatment of women in their adversary's country to ridicule each other's human rights record. Neither country has much to crow about.

Iranians had ample reason to be angry at their regime besides its misogyny. The Iranian economy was doing poorly, a result of sanctions reimposed on the regime by the United States in 2018 (which the United States called its "maximum pressure" campaign), poor economic decision-making, corruption, and the cost of foreign adventures, which many Iranians have come to resent as much as the regime's corruption. As a result, on the eve of the protests, unemployment stood at 11.5 percent, the inflation rate topped 75 percent, and one-third of the population lived in extreme poverty. The value of the Iranian rial declined to such an extent that the government replaced it with a new currency simply so that it might lop four zeros off the denominations of the new bills it issued.

Compounding the economic crisis—as well as Iran's humanitarian crisis—was the government's botched response to the COVID-19 pandemic. This included the government's attempt to substitute a homegrown vaccine for vaccines produced in the United States and the United Kingdom. Those vaccines, according to Khamenei, are "completely untrustworthy. It's not unlikely they would want to contaminate other nations."[11] By the time the government rolled out its own "COVIran Barekat" vaccine and began to import vaccines from Russia, China, and India, the damage to public health and trust in the regime had already been done. From January 2020 through January 2023, 145,000 Iranians died from COVID.

Then there is the brutality, repressive nature, and lack of accountability of the regime. Iran executed 314 prisoners in 2021, and girls as young as nine and boys as young as fifteen can be sentenced to death. The country regularly monitors the Internet and has established a wide network of surveillance, using facial-recognition technology to monitor the activities of its citizens and copycat versions of Google and Instagram to monitor what they read online. Newspapers must be licensed by the state. It censors them and journalists are subject to arrest for writing anti-regime articles or reporting news the government finds derogatory.

While Iran has an elected parliament and an elected president, their functions are mainly administrative. Even then, candidates for office are vetted and their ranks culled by the Council of Guardians, appointed directly and indirectly by the

Supreme Leader. Real power is in his hands and in the hands of the Islamic Revolutionary Guard Corps (IRGC) and the *basij*, its volunteer wing. Their job is to protect the integrity of the Islamic Republic. Like the military in Egypt, the corps plays a major role in the economy and in the distribution of patronage. It is estimated that the IRGC controls one-third of the formal economy and an unknown amount of the underground economy. Hence its power, wealth, and leverage. The Iranian population sees through the democratic charade, of course. That is why only 48.8 percent of eligible voters cast ballots for a presidential candidate in 2021—the lowest percentage in the history of the Islamic Republic.

While the 2022–2023 protests mobilized a broad swath of the Iranian population—shopkeepers and wealthy inhabitants of north Tehran, university students and laborers, Persians and Kurds—there is a reason this episode of resistance would go the way of the 2009, 2017, and 2019 episodes. As had happened before, the 150,000-man IRGC and the 90,000-man basij did not break ranks with the embattled regime—a constancy that saved it.

It might be argued that the initial phases of the Tunisian and Egyptian uprisings succeeded because the men with guns stood down when confronted with mass uprisings of their fellow citizens (as had happened during the Iranian Revolution of 1977–1979). On the other hand, the military in Syria, egged on by a brutal regime that feared for its very existence, deployed increasingly lethal levels of violence until it and its allies felt secure that they had ground down the insurgency. So, too, did the men with guns save the Iranian regime. While some more successful resistance movement might emerge in the future to claim the protests following the death of Mahsa Amini as a harbinger of its triumph, such an outcome was not to be in 2022–2023.

# 4

# PATRONS, PROXIES, AND FREELANCERS

## THE INTERNATIONAL RELATIONS OF THE NEW MIDDLE EAST

### How did the United States become hegemonic in the Middle East?

Anwar al-Sadat, president of Egypt from 1970 to 1981, once quipped that he had switched sides in the Cold War from the Soviet Union to the United States because the United States held "99 percent of the cards in the region."[1] The United States became the hegemonic power in the Middle East not only because it was the dominant economic and military power globally, but because its goals in the region remained consistent for almost half a century, because it had partners in the region who shared the most important of those goals, and because of its default tactical approach there. The end of American hegemony in the Middle East represents the most significant development in the international relations of the region. It is also one of the markers of the transformation of the region from the "old" Middle East to the new. Since the contraction of American influence, regional powers, along with other outside powers, have jockeyed for position, directly and through surrogates, to advance their interests, block the ambitions of rivals and potential rivals, and fill the void left by America's retrenchment.

Overall, there were six goals of American policy in the Middle East during the Cold War. The first, and most important, was the containment of the Soviet Union. The United States sought to prevent the direct expansion of the Soviet Union into the region as well as the spread of its influence there. This was America's global grand strategy and subsumed the others.

Second, the United States sought to assure Western access to oil that, at the beginning of the Cold War, was essential for European and Japanese recovery and prosperity. The United States did not develop its own appetite for Middle Eastern oil until the 1970s. It quickly learned its lesson.

The third goal of US policy was to ensure the peaceful resolution of conflicts and to maintain a regional balance of power. This was to prevent (or mitigate) the polarization of the region into pro-Western and pro-Soviet camps.

To ensure regional stability, the United States promoted stable, if autocratic, pro-Western states in the region. Policymakers believed that if states of the region were strong, and if they fulfilled the aspirations of their populations, they and their populations would resist Soviet blandishments. Policymakers equated hungry people with communist-leaning ones.

The fifth goal of American policy in the region was the preservation of the independence and territorial integrity of the State of Israel. Numerous factors, including ideological and domestic political ones, led to the American-Israeli alliance. Policymakers ultimately saw the strategic value of the alliance, particularly during the frostiest periods of the Cold War.

Finally, the United States sought to protect the sea lanes, lines of communications, and the like, connecting the United States and Europe with Asia. The Middle East is, after all, the *middle* East. Its geographic position alone made it a prize worth fighting for by any power with global pretensions.

As surprising as it may seem during this period of Middle East debacle after Middle East debacle, American policy in the region was mostly successful in advancing American goals. Most important, by the end of the Cold War the United States had virtually locked the Soviet Union out of the Middle East. All the Soviets had to show for themselves were a few scattered allies in the region—Syria, Iraq, the People's Democratic Republic of Yemen (South Yemen)—that were not particularly stable, reliable, or prosperous.

True, the United States had its share of failures, including its loss of Iran in 1979 as a staunch partner. And to meet its goals the United States supported some of the most appalling regimes on earth, became the region's largest arms supplier, abandoned the Kurds and Palestinians to their fates after promising otherwise, and pressured regimes to adopt economic policies that fed corruption and increased income disparities. However, except for its mixed record when it came to bringing about a peaceful resolution of conflicts in the region, the United States achieved what it had set out to achieve.

There were two reasons for this. First, the United States and its partners in the region were bound together by ties of mutual interest. America's partners were as interested as the United States was in maintaining the status quo in the face of internal and external threats, and they cooperated with the United States—often with enthusiasm—in doing so. This was particularly valuable because of the second reason for American success in the region: America's policy of "offshore balancing."

During the Cold War, the United States rarely directly intervened militarily in the Middle East. It didn't have to. Instead, the United States acted as an "offshore balancer." While according its regional partners a protective shield, the United States relied on them to check the ambitions of potentially hostile or disruptive states and non-state actors. In other words, the United States depended on its partners in the region to do the local policing. Pre-revolutionary Iran and Saudi Arabia acted as the "twin pillars" that protected the Gulf and the flow of oil. They contained Iraq. Israel provided for the defense of American interests to the west. It contained Syria.

The United States and its partners thus acted to thwart any changes in individual states as well as the state system, whether they were incited by communist-inspired insurgencies or by unruly neighbors. In the early 1960s, North Yemeni republicans, supported by pro-Soviet Egypt, rebelled against the monarchists who held power. While Saudi Arabia and Jordan sent troops, President John F. Kennedy sent the Saudi king a personal message informing him that the United States would be there to uphold "Saudi Arabian integrity." When the Palestine Liberation Organization (PLO) threatened to over-throw the Jordanian government in 1970, Syrian tanks entered Jordan on the side of the PLO. The Syrian air force, however, did not provide them air cover, because the Israeli air force made its presence over Jordan known. To let the Israelis know the Americans had their back, the American Sixth Fleet steamed to the eastern Mediterranean. In the end, the Jordanian govern-ment prevailed.

There were, of course, a few American military forays into the region. We just couldn't help ourselves. Some of them were successful, some not. The United States intervened in Lebanon twice. The first time was in 1958, when it landed ma-rines there to protect Lebanon from what the Lebanese pres-ident claimed was Egyptian/communist subversion. They secured the port of Beirut and the Beirut airport, but they did not see any action. America's second intervention in Lebanon as part of a multinational force, however, ended disastrously. Originally deployed in 1983 as peacekeepers separating the PLO and Israel, the American troops, mostly marines, suffered 241 fatalities when a suicide bomber blew up the barracks where they were sleeping. The US government ignominiously evacuated the remainder.

With the end of the Cold War the United States lost the ra-tionale for policies that had guided its activities in the Middle East since it had become a superpower. The loss of clear goals and the abandonment of offshore balancing marked the begin-ning of a process that would culminate in the end of American hegemony in the region and spark a struggle among both states and non-state actors to reconstitute the international order there.

### How did the United States lose its hegemonic position in the Middle East?

To continue al-Sadat's gambling metaphor: The United States once held 99 percent of the cards in the Middle East. Then it overplayed its hand. Then it threw in its hand.

In the immediate aftermath of the Cold War, the United States led a military campaign supported by thirty-two countries to evict Iraq from Kuwait, which Iraq had invaded and occupied for reasons analysts still debate. That mission accomplished, the United States withdrew its forces. The Gulf War of 1991 lasted one hundred hours.

The Gulf War was not just a triumph of arms; it was also a marker of a shift in American strategy away from a policy of offshore balancing to one of direct military intervention. During the Iran-Iraq War (1980–1988), the United States had provided satellite intelligence (and maybe more) to the weaker Iraq so that it could continue a fight that preoccupied both countries. This prevented either one from dominating the Persian Gulf or making mischief elsewhere. But during the administration of Bill Clinton, the United States and its allies adopted a "dual containment" policy against Iran and Iraq. Instead of balancing the two states against each other, the United States (and Britain) used airpower to isolate and enforce sanctions against both at the same time. The purpose was either to get the regimes to change their ways or to encourage their overthrow if they did not. Dual containment depended on stationing forces nearby—Saudi Arabia—where the United States had stationed troops during the Gulf War. (American troops on sacred soil was one of the reasons Osama bin Laden gave for plotting the 9/11 attacks.)

The American policymakers who were behind the shift away from the successful strategy of offshore balancing viewed the collapse of the Soviet Union as an opportunity for the world's sole remaining superpower to flex its muscles and shape the world according to its own interests and values. Some, known as neoconservatives, believed the United States could ignore the niceties of international law and international institutions and impose its will unilaterally, by force if necessary. Many of George W. Bush's advisers were "neocons" (that is, neoconservatives). Neocons not only got the United States embroiled in wars in Afghanistan and Iraq they initiated the Global War on Terrorism—a war without end.

Others, known as liberal internationalists, also believed that "American values" should be applied universally but argued that the United States should do this by working within the framework of international law and international institutions. Hillary Clinton, Obama's secretary of state, was one such liberal internationalist. Liberal internationalists were responsible for the United States' participation in the bombing campaign to oust Muammar Qaddafi in Libya during the 2011 uprising there (Madeleine Albright, another liberal internationalist secretary of state, once told the chair of the Joint Chiefs of Staff, "What's the point of having this superb military that you're always talking about if we can't use it?"[2]). They also advocated a more direct American role in the Syrian civil war. Neither campaign had the desired result.

While most Americans were willing to accept the Afghanistan war and the Global War on Terrorism because of their connection to 9/11, the war in Iraq soured them on further adventures in the Middle East. It also demonstrated the limits of American military power—the one power at which the United States excels—to effect decisive solutions to complex problems. Overall, the war in Iraq cost the United States close to 4,500 combat fatalities, more than 32,000 military personnel injured (not including those suffering from posttraumatic stress disorder), $1.7 trillion in war expenses, and $7 trillion in projected interest payments for money borrowed to fight it, not to mention the estimated 184,000 to 207,000 Iraqi dead and the incalculable cost to national self-confidence and international reputation. Certainly, the idea that even a global superpower had the ability to flex its muscles and spread its norms and values took a hit.

None of the US presidents elected since the beginning of the Iraq War would commit to anything near such an adventure again, nor even commit the United States to the same role it had played in the region during the Cold War.

Obama saw the Middle East, with its incessant conflicts, autocratic governments, systemic corruption, and rent-seeking economics, as a place that was more trouble than it was worth for the United States. For Obama, America's post–Cold War obsession with the Middle East is like an amputee scratching an itch on a phantom limb. That is why he attempted to extricate the United States from the region, wind down America's endless wars there, put a lid on potential hot spots—the Israel-Palestine conflict, the Saudi-Iranian rivalry—before they boiled over, and "pivot to Asia." Asia was the region that was destined to be at the geostrategic fulcrum in the twenty-first century. (Joe Biden, Obama's vice president, quietly embraced Obama's policies when he became president.) That is also why Obama expended enormous amounts of political capital nudging reluctant Israelis toward a settlement with Palestinians, negotiating a deal that would constrain Iran's nuclear program, and "leading [America's NATO allies] from behind"[3] in Libya while refusing to pick up the pieces when Libya unraveled.

Obama was only partially successful in lessening America's footprint in the region. Not only did some policies just plain fail, but American policymakers were also blindsided by events, some of which they could not have foreseen, others of which wishful thinking or obtuseness prevented them from seeing. The former category included not only the Arab uprisings, the Syrian civil war, and the rise of ISIS, but also the Turkish drift to authoritarianism and Russian assertion. The latter included the Israeli pushback against a freeze on settlement expansion on Palestinian land and the Saudi pushback against any number of American policies. Unfortunately, policymakers did not prove themselves particularly nimble when confronted by errant events, nor were there any guideposts for them to follow in this brave new world. In the end, the pivot failed.

Like Obama, Donald Trump wanted to extricate the United States from its military commitments in the Middle East (and elsewhere). Hence, the slogan "America first." But that is where the similarities of their policies end. While it might be said that Obama's strategic vision was too intricate to be practicable, Trump's strategic vision was non-existent. Guided by impulse, the promise of political gain, a reverence for strongmen, and boundless appetite to upend all of Obama's policies (what a former British ambassador to United States called "diplomatic vandalism"[4]), Trump delegated American policy in the region to Israel and Saudi Arabia and made their ambitions and obsessions—particularly the Iranian "threat"—his own. In the end, the contradictions between "America first" and a bellicose Iran policy (Trump not only renounced the Iran nuclear accord but ordered the assassination of one of the leaders of Iran's Revolutionary Guard Corps) sowed confusion among America's friends and adversaries. Even Saudi Arabia decided its best bet would be to bypass its uncertain ally and negotiate with Iran to see if it might not lower the temperature in the region.

In July 2022, Biden addressed representatives of the GCC meeting in Saudi Arabia. "We will not walk away and leave a vacuum to be filled by China, Russia, or Iran," he said. "And we'll seek to build on this moment with active, principled American leadership."[5] Although Biden did not specify what form that leadership might take, chances are the United States has lost its hegemonic position in the Middle East for good. Policy analysts and historians will continue to argue about whether that loss was inevitable, the result of accidental factors, or the result of the failings of one or another leader (George W. Bush? Barack Obama?). But in the end, it is worth remembering the unique set of circumstances that both permitted and compelled the United States to take on the role of Middle East hegemon and that obliged states in the region to accept it as such.

During the period of American hegemony in the Middle East, the global system was bipolar, the contest to dominate the region played out as a zero sum game in which a victory for one side meant a loss for the other, and the Middle East was a prize worth competing for. The United States was unrivaled as an economic and, arguably, military power and had a preeminent position within the global economic system. There was a core group of states in the Middle East whose interests aligned with American interests and whose very existence the American security umbrella guaranteed. And with the help of some deft diplomacy in the wake of the 1973 Arab-Israeli War, the United States became the only power capable of brokering a land-for-peace deal among the combatants. This put the most populous and militarily capable Arab state, Egypt—previously the region's preeminent spoiler—permanently in the American pocket.

Comparable circumstances no longer exist.

### Will China take America's place as Middle East hegemon?

Who, if anyone, will take on the role of hegemon in the Middle East? Before Russia's disastrous campaign in Ukraine—when Russia had just come off its "successful" intervention in Syria by leveling Aleppo from the height of more than 13,000 feet—some suggested that it would replace the United States as the hegemonic power in the region. A 2017 RAND Corporation report on Russia's ambitions in the Middle East, however, underscores why this is not likely to occur. The report uses some variation on the word "transactional" sixteen times and "opportunistic" or "opportunity" eighteen times within the space of eleven pages to describe the bases for Russian policy in the region. It then goes on to conclude that "Russia potentially lacks the economic and military power to sustain a long-term strategy"[6] Obama agrees. He once dismissed America's Cold War rival as a "regional power" that acts out of weakness, not strength.[7] Russia's disastrous attempt to create a puppet state in Ukraine while the world looked on confirms Obama's skepticism about Russian capabilities.

Others have suggested Europe. The section of the European Union's 2016 strategic program dealing with the Middle East begins with a call to action: "solving conflicts and promoting development and human rights in the south is essential to addressing the threat of terrorism, the challenges of demography, migration and climate change, and to seizing the opportunity of shared prosperity."[8] But the program then veers off course, ignoring what it said previously and abdicating primary responsibility to regional actors while relegating Europe to a supporting role. Europe's short-term focus on migration has made it a supplicant rather than a leader when dealing with Middle Eastern regimes. The refugee crisis has put Europe at the mercy of Turkey and Libya.

The most commonly cited contender for hegemon to replace the United States is China. In 2013, Chinese president Xi Jinping announced China's Belt and Road Initiative (BRI). The initiative—the largest development project in history—would link China's prosperous coast with its less prosperous western and southwestern regions and, through both land and sea routes, with South and Southeast Asia, Central Asia, the Middle East, Europe, and Latin America. Loans from Chinese state-operated enterprises, commercial and "policy" banks (China's export-import and agricultural banks), and various ministries go to the construction of infrastructure, including ports, railroads, high-speed internet, power plants, telecommunications, and the like in those areas. This will solve two problems for the Chinese: linking poor and restive regions of the country with China's boom towns, and expanding the global pipeline for the export of manufactured goods and import of raw materials.

Twenty Middle East countries have signed up for the initiative or have expressed their approval for it. Little wonder: with its decentralized lending institutions and lack of oversight, the BRI is catnip for authoritarians worldwide seeking enrichment for themselves and their cronies. The fear among some analysts, however, is that Chinese economic investment will lead to Chinese geopolitical and diplomatic assertion, filling the void left by a detached and spent United States in the Middle East. That scenario is unlikely. The Chinese are not oblivious to the American experience in the region, which has been less than auspicious. Furthermore, their interests (oil, shipping lanes) can best be served if they do not have to pick and choose sides among regional competitors, particularly since the three largest suppliers of oil to China are, in ranked order, Saudi Arabia, Iraq, and Iran. And even though Chinese foreign policy has been more assertive of late, China has limited its assertiveness to its own "near abroad"—the South China Sea and its immediate neighbors.

There is no reason that China should shoulder the responsibilities of a hegemon when it can take advantage of existing security networks and a functioning global economic system sustained by others, as it has in the past. China's role in the contemporary Middle East is, ironically, similar to the role played by the United States in the region during the period between the two world wars. American companies came to dominate the global trade in oil while others—Britain and France—paid the price of hegemons, bearing the cost of providing the stability that enabled the activities of those companies.

Thus, for those who would ask, "Will China replace the United States as Middle East hegemon?" the answer is "Why should it?" Chinese officials have said that the future of the Middle East will be multipolar, without a single hegemon. There is little reason to doubt their word. Such an "open-door policy" was America's policy as well during its rise to global economic prominence.

### How has the relationship between the United States and its partners changed since the Cold War?

During the Cold War, the fundamental interest of the United States and its partners—preventing the disruption of the status quo by any state or non-state actor—coincided. Although there were some issues upon which there were differing opinions— the conflict between Israel and the Arab world, a consistent bone of contention, and, intermittently, oil policy and human rights—mutual interest overrode discord and diplomats chose to "delink" those issues from wider concerns.

After the collapse of the Soviet Union, that overriding mutual interest was gone, and the United States and its partners diverged in terms of what they considered to be their national interests and how to go about achieving them.

For example, America's Arab partners grew accustomed to American support no matter what they did domestically. So even though the support the United States gave to the Arab uprisings was tepid (with the exception of Libya), the fact that the United States did not go to the mat for autocrats it had once supported shocked and angered them. That can be seen in the well-worn but false Saudi refrain that the United States had thrown Hosni Mubarak under a bus (in fact, while the Obama administration policy was evolving from continued support of Mubarak to calling for a transition government that would include him, the Egyptian people were busy throwing him under a bus). And when Bashar al-Assad used chemical weapons on his own people—thus crossing America's self-proclaimed "red line"—and the United States inflicted no punishment on him for doing so, the Saudis (and others) were apoplectic that the United States had refrained from involving itself directly in the Syrian imbroglio.

It is not just in the Arab world where American interests and the interests of its partners in the region—both real and perceived—diverged. Take Israel. The Obama administration, like almost every administration since the time of Dwight D. Eisenhower, subscribed to the doctrine of "linkage." Those who believe in linkage believe that instability in the Middle East is ultimately "linked" to a failure to resolve the Israel-Palestine conflict. Therefore, resolving the conflict became an imperative for administration after administration—that is, until each administration got burned and moved on.

Over the years, however, Israel became more right wing, nationalistic, and religiously orthodox than it had been before the 1967 war. During the war, Israel came to occupy the Palestinian territories, and what to do with those territories came to occupy the center stage of Israeli politics. In the 1980s, Israeli politicians on the right formed an alliance with the so-called settler movement, which is composed of those Israelis who want to retain and "settle"—colonize—the territories. They balked at making any agreement brokered by the United States that might force Israel to disgorge them. Thus, short-term political calculus trumped what American policymakers, rightly or wrongly, believed to be in America's (and Israel's) national interest.

Currently, Israel, like Saudi Arabia, views Iran—particularly a nuclear-armed Iran—as an existential threat. It has reason. Not only has Iran supported Hizbullah, a former Iranian president once quoted Iran's first post-revolution leader as stating that Israel "must be wiped out from the map of the world."[9] Israel, like Saudi Arabia, did what it could to scuttle the nuclear deal that the so-called P5 + 1 countries (members of the UN Security Council plus the European Union) brokered with Iran. For them, it was not strong enough because it did not dismantle Iran's nuclear program in its entirety; rather, it delayed and diminished it. Both countries urged the United States not to sign the deal; instead, they urged the United States to take other steps—including military action, if necessary—to prevent Iran from enriching weapons-grade uranium. The Israeli prime minister at the time, Benjamin Netanyahu, even bypassed the president of the United States and took his case directly to the US Congress.

The United States signed the deal anyway. The Obama administration perceived nuclear proliferation to be not only a threat to the peace of the region, but an existential threat to the United States. It certainly did not want a nuclear arms race in the Middle East.

Then there is Turkey, a NATO ally and a state that has become increasingly autocratic, particularly after an attempted coup d'état in July 2016 gave Turkish president Recep Tayyip Erdogan (pronounced AIR-da-wan) the pretext to clamp down on his opponents. Like Saudi Arabia, Turkey has backed some unsavory groups in Syria. As a matter of fact, Turkey and the United States have nurtured relationships with two very different varieties of groups in the Syrian civil war: Turkey has worked closely with the Islamist opposition, and the United States with Kurdish groups. Turkey views those groups as an existential threat. It believes their quest for an autonomous or independent Syrian Kurdistan might inspire Turkey's own Kurds to seek the same. The United States, however, has depended on the Kurds in its war against ISIS.

As in the case of Saudi Arabia and Israel, there is little likelihood Turkey will sever its long-standing relationship with the country that is still the world's foremost military and economic power. There are too many shared interests—from the economic and political to the institutional—binding them together. There have been rough patches in America's relationship with all three before: the king of Saudi Arabia, incensed by comments made by George W. Bush about tilting toward Israel in the Israeli-Palestinian conflict, refused an invitation to visit him; the United States has opposed Israeli military actions and settlement activities on a number of occasions; and the United States slapped an arms embargo on Turkey after it invaded Cyprus in 1974.

Nevertheless, since Saudi Arabia, Israel, and Turkey perceive their interests as conflicting with American interests in a variety of realms, those relationships may prove to be rockier in the future than in the past.

### What are the roots of the Saudi-Iranian competition?

The most significant regional divide in the New Middle East remains the one that separates Saudi Arabia and its allies from Iran and its. Among Saudi Arabia's allies are most states in the Arab world and, unofficially, Israel. Among Iran's are Syria, Hizbullah, and the Houthis of Yemen. Since the outbreak of the Arab uprisings in 2010, Saudi Arabia and Iran have been on opposite sides in a number of civil conflicts and political disputes.

- The Iranians support Hizbullah in Lebanon. In addition to the shared goal of keeping Israel off balance, leaders from Iran and Hizbullah have built personal relationships dating back to the days when they studied theology together at the shrine cities of Najaf and Karbala in Iraq. The Iranians have used Syria as a land bridge to arm Hizbullah and have provided it with sophisticated missiles that the group has used against Israel. Iranian support for Hizbullah, however, has driven the Saudis apoplectic. The Saudis forced the resignation of Lebanese prime minister Saad Hariri, a longtime ally, while he was visiting Riyadh to force the collapse of Hariri's government, which included Hizbullah (he rescinded his resignation once he was safely out of the kingdom). The Saudis later broke off diplomatic relations with Lebanon when a cabinet minister whose party was aligned with Hizbullah called the Saudi participation in the Yemen conflict against the Iranian-linked Houthis "absurd."
- In Iraq, the Iranians have thrown their weight behind a number of Shi'i politicians, including Nouri al-Maliki,

who served as prime minister from 2006 to 2014, along with various Shi'i parties and militias involved in the fight against ISIS. The Saudis considered al-Maliki to be an Iranian agent and disapproved strongly of his Shi'i-dominated government. Beginning in 2014, the Saudis decided that sitting on the sidelines in Iraq was self-defeating. They began a charm offensive to unite anti-Iranian Sunni and Shi'i politicians who feared lest Iran turn Iraq into a wholly owned subsidiary of the Islamic Republic.

• The Saudis saw an Iranian footprint in the Bahraini up-rising of 2011, where it did not exist, took the side of the opposition against the Iranian-backed regime in Syria, and launched a war in Yemen to fight the Houthi insurgency, claiming that Iran was behind it. Most commentators note that the Houthi insurgency, which began in 2004, was stirred by local grievances and that initially the Iranian role was minimal.

• The Saudis have also confronted Iran diplomatically. The Saudis opposed the P5 + 1 deal with the Iranians, fearing that it would bring Iran out of isolation. Saudi Arabia also opposed tiny Qatar's balancing act between its two larger neighbors and led an international move-ment to boycott it (the boycott ended in 2021). And after Iranians stormed the Saudi embassy in Tehran (incited by the Saudi execution of a prominent Saudi Shi'i cleric), the Saudis not only broke off diplomatic relations with Iran, they "encouraged" Bahrain, Kuwait, the UAE, and Sudan to downgrade or cut ties also.

A number of commentators trace the Saudi-Iranian com-petition in the region to the Sunni-Shi'i split that divided the Islamic community after the death of Muhammad in AD 632 (Shi'ism as a separate sect dates from about 130 years later). History, however, tells us something different. There have been long periods of time when Shi'is and Sunnis lived together without problems. In fact, at the time of the American invasion of Iraq, marriages between Sunnis and Shi'is represented approximately 30 percent of all marriages there. Sectarianism is not the universal default position for Muslims. It is no more natural for Muslims to fuse their religious identity with their political identity than it is for anyone else to do so. Sectarianism can always be traced to political entrepreneurs who transform communal solidarity into a demand for rights, set-asides, or even autonomy. Those entrepreneurs might be individuals, groups and parties, or even governments.

There have been times when governments of Sunni-dominated lands shared interests and cooperated with governments of Shi'i-dominated lands. Before the Iranian Revolution, both Saudi Arabia and Iran supported American policy in the Gulf. After the revolution, Iran allied itself with Hamas, the (Sunni) Palestinian group that dominates Gaza in its confrontation with Israel (since Hamas allied itself with the opposition in Syria, relations have not been as close as they used to be). And the bloodiest war of the post–World War II period pitted Iran against Iraq—two predominantly Shi'i states. In spite of predictions to the contrary, Shi'is living in Iraq and Sunnis (and Arabs) living in Iran remained loyal to their respective governments.

If the hostility between Saudi Arabia and Iran were a dispute between Sunnis and Shi'is, one would expect Sunni Turkey to ally itself with Sunni Saudi Arabia against Shi'i Iran. Of course, Turkey and Iran *have been* on opposite sides in the Syrian civil war, and Turkey often *does* have good relations with the states of the GCC. Nevertheless, Turkey and Iran are currently enjoying cordial relations, while Saudi-Turkish relations fluctuate with the season. Turkey and Iran enjoy a strong economic relationship, and both oppose Kurdish aspirations, which, they believe, threaten the integrity of their countries. Alternatively, while Turkey supported various Muslim Brotherhood movements during the 2010–2011 uprisings, the

Saudis opposed them, believing them to be an ideological and political threat to the kingdom.

If the current Saudi-Iranian animosity is not about religion per se, what, then, is it about? Simply put, it's about politics. Saudi Arabia and Iran (along with Turkey) operate on different models of governance, have different goals in the region, and have different survival strategies.

Saudi Arabia promotes submission to the dynasty at home and adherence to the status quo abroad. The Saudi government does not like to see Islamic activism anywhere because it threatens that status quo. Hence, its opposition not only to an "Islamic Republic" but to Muslim Brotherhood parties and governments throughout the region, which provide a model for harnessing Islam to politics in a way that the Saudi government opposes and fears. Saudi Arabia has also been aligned with the United States, the dominant status quo power in the world that has acted as the ultimate guarantor of the Middle East state system.

The profile of Iran is the polar opposite of that of Saudi Arabia. A staunch ally of the United States in the region before the revolution of 1978–1979, Iran flipped its foreign policy 180 degrees after it.

The newly established Islamic Republic viewed itself as a revolutionary power intent on shaking up the status quo and defying and rolling back American imperialism. While in its rhetoric and actions it has largely backed away from spreading its revolutionary model, it has taken advantage of cracks in the system, particularly those that might be traced to the Arab uprisings. Iran's reach has been exaggerated by Saudi Arabia— what better way for the Saudis to rally domestic and foreign support than to raise a cry of alarm? Nevertheless, Iran has responded positively to the 2010–2011 uprisings and protests (with the notable exception of Syria) that have challenged the old order in the Arab world. That old order has involved the oppression of Shi'is in a number of places in the region (including Saudi Arabia's Eastern Province, where the kingdom's oil is located). Iran thus has had both causes to champion and groups to which it could appeal on the basis of communal solidarity.

Nevertheless, while both Saudi Arabia and Iran have, since 2010, played the sectarian card to gain allies and thus advantage in their struggle for dominance, the Saudis have played it more aggressively than the Iranians. This only stands to reason. Beginning with the Obama administration, the Saudis felt more vulnerable than ever before—whether that feeling was justified or not.

Before Obama, Saudi Arabia counted on the United States to be there if an existential threat arose. When Obama was in office, the Saudis suspected the American commitment to their defense and feared abandonment. With Obama as president, the Saudi stance in the face of danger was no longer, as it had been since the 1990s, to crawl under the table and wait for the arrival of the American cavalry. Saudi Arabia became proactive financially, diplomatically, and militarily, against the wishes of the United States (under Obama and Biden) or with America's blessing (under Trump).

In addition, the Arab uprisings fed Saudi feelings of vulnerability because they threaten or have threatened to upset the status quo. Saudi Arabia has seen the governments of close allies, such as Bahrain and Yemen, endangered or removed, and its own under threat. And it has not just been the uprisings that have threatened the balance in the region. Although there was no love lost between Saudi Arabia and Saddam Hussein, his replacement by a Shi'i-dominated government and its inability to act as a counterbalance against Iran has been a bitter pill to swallow.

### Will Saudi Arabia and Iran reconcile?

In March 2023, Saudi Arabia and Iran agreed to restore diplomatic relations, which they had severed in 2016. They also agreed to refrain from provocative acts against each other that might lead to all-out conflict.

The fact that Saudi Arabia and Iran reached this agreement in Beijing provided fodder for commentators who cited it as more evidence that China was on the road to becoming the next hegemon in the Middle East. Saudi Arabia and Iran hardly needed Chinese mediation, however. Representatives from each country had met multiple times, largely in Oman and Iraq, and Saudi Arabia was following in the footsteps of the UAE and Kuwait, both of which had quietly restored diplomatic relations with Iran in 2022. In other words, both Saudi Arabia and Iran had already signaled that they were committed to finding a way to reduce tensions. China could take center stage because it had diplomatic and trade relations with both countries, which the United States did not.

And it didn't hurt that holding the signing ceremony in Beijing enabled all three to ruffle American feathers—something they all wanted to do, if for different reasons—by giving the former hegemon the cold shoulder.

The term many of these commentators used for the agreement was *rapprochement*—diplospeak for reconciliation. There is, however, a more accurate word used in diplomacy, also French, to describe what was occurring between Saudi Arabia and Iran: *détente* (the relaxing of tension).

Diplomats of a previous generation used *rapprochement* to refer to the warming up of America's relationship with (Communist) China during the Cold War, when both countries sought to present a united front against the Soviet Union by working together. Diplomats used *détente*, on the other hand, to refer to attempts to post guardrails that would prevent a devastating nuclear war between the United States and the Soviet Union while the two countries continued to compete against each other in remote corners of the globe. Thus, during the period of *détente* (1969–1979), the United States and the Soviet Union signed treaties limiting the deployment of strategic weapons that might be used to blow each other up. At the same time, the United States assisted Israel and the Soviet Union assisted Egypt and Syria during the 1973 Arab-Israeli War—the bloodiest of all Arab-Israeli wars.

In the wake of three American administrations the Saudis regarded as unreliable, they came to believe they could not depend on unconditional American support against Iran. In addition, Saudi crown prince Muhammad bin Salman had big domestic plans for Saudi Arabia, which war with Iran would have upended. For their part, the Iranians were isolated internationally and faced economic and political turmoil internally. Avoiding direct conflict while attending to other matters thus suited both sides. Although *rapprochement* between a power that supports the status quo and one that is equally determined to overturn it might have been impossible, both could take a few steps back from the precipice.

That is, for as long as the agreement lasts.

### What role will oil play in the New Middle East?

From June 2014 to April 2016, oil prices dropped 70 percent. Economists gave a number of reasons for the drop. Some pointed to temporary aberrations. One such aberration was a downturn in the Chinese economy, which decreased demand in the world's second-largest consumer of imported oil. Another was deliberate Saudi overproduction to drive oil prices down in order to hurt the economies of Saudi Arabia's Russian and Iranian competitors. Perhaps the most troubling long-term news for oil exporters, however, came from the United States. New technologies, such as horizontal drilling and fracking (breaking up subterranean rock to release oil and natural gas) made the United States the world's largest oil producer. And while the United States increased production, domestic demand in the world's largest oil consumer also fell. American oil consumption was lower in 2015 than it had been in 1997, mainly as a result of increased fuel efficiency in cars.

That holy grail of American politics, energy independence, seemed at last to be within reach.

After 2016, the price of oil rebounded, then began to gyrate up and down in response to other aberrations. It went down in 2020 as a result of the COVID-19 pandemic, lockdowns, and a global economic downturn. It went up again as the world grew accustomed to dealing with COVID-19, as governments pumped more money into their economies, as the largest producers agreed to lower supply, and as the war in Ukraine created uncertainty in markets. Russia, one of the world's largest producers, imposed targeted supply cutoffs as well.

By that time, however, oil producers in the Gulf and Saudi Arabia had decided to get off the roller coaster and find a more consistent income stream. Some had already begun to diversify their economies. Qatar and the UAE, for example, invested in finance, real estate, construction, tourism, and even manufacturing. All remained oil dependent, however, and a number of them decided to go back to the drawing board and figure out ways to wean themselves off oil dependency once and for all. The years of low oil prices thus coincided with years of economic development plans, or "visions": Vision 2021 (the UAE), National Vision 2030 (Qatar), Vision 2030 (Saudi Arabia), Vision 2035 (Kuwait), and Vision 2040 (Oman).

These plans were similar in nature. In accordance with the advice of the IMF, they called for oil producers to bolster science, technology, and vocational education; target specific sectors and industries for investment (the financial sector in Bahrain, petrochemicals and mining in Saudi Arabia); invest in infrastructure; strengthen their legal and regulatory environment; and encourage entrepreneurship and innovation by expanding access to information. In theory, this would stimulate the private sector and move Saudi Arabia and the Gulf countries toward an export model like that of Japan or Korea.

Take, for example, the Saudi Vision 2030,[10] unveiled by then–Deputy Crown Prince Muhammad bin Salman (now the crown prince) in spring 2016. This particular vision was prepared by an American consulting firm, McKinsey & Co., and is more of a retread than a vision. In fact, Vision 2030 includes a list of off-the-shelf neo-liberal recommendations that might just as well have been prepared for the government of Peru. The plan calls for privatizing government assets, including education and 5 percent of the national oil company, Saudi Aramco; reducing and targeting subsidies on oil, electricity, and water; introducing an income tax; investing in tourism and entertainment; and reducing unemployment, increasing female participation in the workforce, and creating 450,000 new private-sector jobs.

The crown jewel of Vision 2030 is the construction of a new urban complex on the Red Sea—Neom (the name comes from a combination of the Greek word for "new" and the first letter of the Arabic word for "future")—that will include a smart, linear city ("The Line") stretching 110 miles long, 1,600 feet tall, and 700 feet wide, built to house nine million people. It will come replete with flying taxis, robot maids, and an artificial moon. The initial costs are $500 billion.

Other states in the region have also begun construction of new cities. Kuwait has its "Silk City" in its north; the UAE, its Masdar City. But pushing the envelope is one thing; fantasy another. And the construction of a new Brasilia that will use technologies that do not yet exist is perfectly in line with the quixotic nature of much of the rest of Vision 2030.

Parts of the plan have already taken hits. The government had to give up on its plans for an income tax, relying instead on hidden taxes such as a value-added tax and import taxes that are less likely to stir resentment. And the international community has shown little confidence in a crown prince who expands his power in the name of liberalization while ruthlessly quashing dissent. In 2017 the government rounded up one hundred princes and other billionaires, "jailed" them in the Ritz-Carlton on trumped-up corruption charges and only released them after it had shaken them down for $100 billion. The brutal assassination of a dissident journalist,

Jamal Khashoggi, who was lured into the Saudi consulate in Istanbul—likely on orders of the crown prince himself—further estranged the international community, at least temporarily.

In the end, the government was forced to restrict sale of shares of Saudi Aramco to Saudi nationals—and by 2022 investors had bought only 1.5 percent of the shares in the company, not five.

Vision 2030 will likely go the way of the nine other development plans Saudi Arabia has published since 1970. Its promise to wean Saudi Arabia off its oil dependency will remain unfulfilled. For Saudi Arabia to become globally competitive in less than two decades means unilaterally redefining the ruling bargain that connects the Saudi population with its government. It means discarding the most effective tool the government has for gaining the consent of its population—buying it. It means ensuring a free flow of information in a country that, in 2022, Reporters without Borders ranked 166th out of 180 countries surveyed in terms of press freedom—a country in which transparency on all levels of governance and commerce is rare. And it means changing attitudes toward work in a country in which women make up only 33 percent of the workforce (the global average in 2020 was 47 percent) and foreigners literally do all the heavy lifting.

### How have relations among states changed in the New Middle East?

The Westphalian System is named after the site of treaty negotiations that ended the Thirty Years' War, in 1648. Although many historians dispute the connection between the treaty and the system, "Westphalian System" has become shorthand for the fundamental principle of international relations: the inviolability of sovereign states. In other words, states are not to interfere in the internal affairs of other states.

If only it were that simple. Great powers like the United States have often ignored legal norms when it suited their

needs. For example, the United States supported the first post–
World War II coup d'état in the Arab world, which took place
in Syria. Then came what was, perhaps, its most famous covert
intervention in the region. Four years after the Syria coup, the
Americans, along with the British, organized and financed the
overthrow of the legally elected prime minister of Iran, who
had the temerity to nationalize Iran's oil industry. Any account of America's violation of sovereign rights in the region
must also include George W. Bush's ongoing Global War on
Terrorism—rhetorically downgraded by Obama to "overseas
contingency operations." The "war" justified military strikes
and assassinations against select targets, frequently without
the knowledge or permission of the governments of states in
which they take place.

   In 2005, the UN Security Council adopted a resolution
establishing as an international norm a doctrine known as
Responsibility to Protect (R2P). After the failure of multiple
humanitarian interventions in the 1990s, the international
community formally recognized the principle that the protection of civilian lives imperiled by natural disasters or atrocities
was an international responsibility and that the international
community might use any number of tools, from sanctions
to military intervention, to do so—even if it meant violating
a nation's sovereign rights. The Security Council resolution
that authorized the air campaign against Qaddafi's forces in
Libya explicitly cited the doctrine. When the campaign led
to the capture and execution of Qaddafi, critics charged that
R2P had merely been diplomatic cover for regime change. It
is doubtful that Russia and China will support invoking the
doctrine again.

   While the use of R2P in Libya was anomalous, the post-2011
abandonment of the principles of respect for state sovereignty
and non-intervention in the Middle East has not been. Powers
great and small, from inside and outside the region, have
seemingly thrown caution to the wind and abandoned the
Westphalian playbook. This is because of the presence in the

region of widespread civil disorder, state breakdown, and intense interstate competition, on the one hand, and the absence in the region of a hegemon that might have reserved such transgressions for itself, on the other. Indeed, with America's Global War on Terrorism, its invasion of Iraq, and the UN Security Council's invocation of R2P, such practices were practically codified. Even the fig leaf of international approval for a state's blatant misconduct seems almost superfluous and quaint.

At one time or another since 2011, Saudi Arabia, the UAE, Qatar, Egypt, Turkey, and Iran, not to mention the United States, its European allies, and Russia, have intervened in one way or another in the internal affairs of Syria, Lebanon, Libya, Iraq, and Yemen against established governments or without their express approval. The case of the UAE—dubbed "Little Sparta" by former US Secretary of Defense James Mattis—is particularly telling.

Enriched by high oil prices that preceded their 2014 collapse, and seemingly set adrift by an America determined to pivot to Asia, the UAE adopted a proactive foreign policy to further its interests. Those interests included parrying the threat from Iran, preventing Muslim Brotherhoods from replacing friendly autocrats in the post-2011 Arab world (the UAE's attitude toward Muslim Brotherhoods was in line with Saudi Arabia's), and securing the UAE's position as a "nexus state"—that is, the indispensable center for finance and commerce linking Europe, the Arabian Gulf, the Indian Ocean, and East Asia.

- Parrying Iran entailed sending military and military-style assistance to the government of Bahrain and the Hadi government in Yemen, where, the UAE government claimed, Iran was inciting insurrections. It entailed joining with Saudi Arabia and other Gulf states in sanctioning Qatar for attempting to balance its relations with the GCC and Iran. It entailed taking steps to bring Syria back into the Arab fold in order to wean Bashar al-Assad from his Iran dependence (the Arab League welcomed Syria back in spring 2023). And it entailed normalizing relations with Israel, another state that viewed Iran as an existential threat.

- The UAE supported Abdel Fattah el-Sisi's coup d'état against the legally elected Muslim Brotherhood government of Egypt in 2013. It probably underwrote the protest movement that mobilized against the government immediately before the coup, then transferred $6 billion in funds to Egypt's central bank after Sisi took power (Saudi Arabia and Kuwait contributed another $12 billion). The UAE has also supported Khalifa Haftar's LNA in Libya against the internationally recognized government there, with which various Islamist groups are affiliated. The UAE has conducted airstrikes on his army's behalf, supplied tons of weapons, and even hired mercenaries to fight alongside the LNA.
- To secure the UAE's position as a nexus state, the UAE opened up a new conflict zone in the Red Sea. The UAE is particularly concerned about assuring navigation through the Bab al-Mandeb chokepoint that connects the sea to the Gulf of Aden and the Arabian Sea. To this end, the UAE has established military bases and supported militias on both sides of the sea. It has used these militias to counter piracy on the Somalia side of Red Sea and to maintain a foothold on the Yemen side. It has also supported regional groupings against central governments in both places. It deals directly with the autonomous Somaliland and Puntland regions of Somalia, much to the annoyance of the Mogadishu government, and sponsored the Southern Transitional Council in Yemen, a collection of secessionist groups that would reestablish South Yemen as a UAE puppet state.

If the Southern Transition Council succeeds, it would mean that Yemen would become the only state in the region to fragment in the wake of the uprisings of 2011. The international community much prefers failed states to shattered ones.

Little Sparta, like a number of its neighbors, has been very busy in the New Middle East.

### What is Turkey's role in the New Middle East?

The parliamentary election of 2002 was a watershed moment in Turkish politics. The Justice and Development Party, at the time heralded as a moderate Islamist party, won two-thirds of the seats, and its leader, Recep Erdogan, became prime minister. Not only did this victory signal another step in the death march of Kemalism—the secular nationalism that was the official ideology since the birth of the republic—it marked a transformation of Turkish foreign policy.

During the previous decades, Turkey had oriented toward the West, and Turkey's grand ambition was to join the European Union as a full member. While Turkey's new government did not abandon this ambition, it also sought to strengthen ties with its neighbors in the Middle East and Caucasus. This policy was called the "zero problems with neighbors" policy. The Turkish government reached out to its Arab neighbors, Russia, Iran, and even its old nemesis, Armenia (to no avail). Some even talked of a New Ottomanism, an orientation that recalled the Istanbul-based empire that governed Anatolia, the Asiatic Arab world, and Egypt until its demise in 1922.

Then came the Arab uprisings of 2010–2011 and a reassessment of the "zero problems" policy. Unlike Saudi Arabia, which viewed the uprisings as a calamity in the making, the Turkish government viewed them as an opportunity to promote like-minded moderate Islamic populist regimes throughout the region. This would buy Turkey influence there. Only tiny Qatar went along with Turkish support for Muslim Brotherhoods, apparently believing that if it didn't ride the Muslim Brotherhood wave, it would drown beneath it. Turkey was thus an early supporter of the short-lived Muslim Brotherhood government in Egypt, Islamist groups in the Syrian opposition, and the GNA in Libya. Turkey's interventions in the bloody aftermath of the Arab uprisings of 2010–2011 thus put it, at one time or another, at odds with Saudi Arabia, the UAE, Egypt, and Syria, as well as others further afield. "Zero problems" had morphed into something decidedly different.

Other policies that seemed to be good ideas at the time reinforced Turkish isolation. For example, in 2010 Turkey broke off diplomatic relations with Israel after Israeli commandos assaulted a Turkish-owned ship, killing ten Turkish citizens. The ship, sailing in international waters, was carrying humanitarian assistance and construction materials to Palestinians in Gaza. Since then, Turkey and Israel restored ties, broke them again, then restored them again. And Israel was not the only state experiencing erratic relations with Turkey. Erdogan's newly found assertiveness managed to get Turkey into spats with a number of other countries as well—including, remarkably enough, the United States under Trump—over issues they might have finessed in a more congenial time. And Erdogan's attempt to straddle both sides in the Ukraine war—political support for Ukraine, continued economic ties with Russia, resistance to Sweden's joining NATO—won him no plaudits from the Western alliance which counts Turkey as a member.

Most troublesome was Turkey's aggressive stance in the Mediterranean, where Turkey had been locked out of the bounty from the sea's largest natural-gas field, discovered in 2015. Not one to take no for an answer, Erdogan signed an agreement with the GNA in Libya to create an exclusive economic zone in what the two states improbably call their joint territorial waters, which stretch from southern Anatolia to North Africa. This zone would intersect the main gas pipeline connecting Cyprus and Greece. Turkey has defended the zone aggressively, disrupting Cypriot oil exploration, buzzing Greek islands with fighter jets, and, of course, defending the GNA from Haftar's LNA. Turkey single-handedly took on the littoral powers and the European Union. In the process, it expanded the Middle East zone of conflict to the greater Mediterranean region.

After the military's abortive coup d'état against Erdogan in 2016, he staged a referendum on a new constitution and, after it won, took office as president. Erdogan's authoritarian streak placed him at the center of power. This meant that he became the focus of acclaim when things went well and the target for blame when they didn't. Erdogan's muscular foreign policy, which seemed to enhance Turkey's regional and global stature, played well at home. But when one oversees an export-oriented economy one must tread carefully. By mid-2022, the Turkish economy was in shambles, chiefly the result of misguided economic policies that drove the inflation rate to about 80 percent. Contributing to the crisis was the collapse of exports and foreign investment, for which an equally misguided foreign policy was responsible. Exports to Saudi Arabia fell by 95 percent in one year. Erdogan's only recourse to save his future was mending fences. And that is precisely what he attempted to do.

It is unlikely that Turkey will abandon its core foreign-policy concerns, such as the Kurdish issue. But whatever the bombast, it is also unlikely that Turkey will again play the sort of role in the New Middle East that Erdogan had once envisioned.

### Whatever happened to the Israel-Palestine conflict?

In 2002, Saudi Arabia proposed an Arab-Israeli, Israeli-Palestinian peace plan it called the "Arab peace initiative." Among other things, the plan called for the complete Israeli withdrawal from all the territories it had conquered in 1967 and the establishment of a Palestinian state in the West Bank and Gaza with East Jerusalem as its capital. If the Israelis were to agree to the proposal, the members of the Arab League would end their states of belligerence with Israel and establish normal relations with it within the framework of a comprehensive peace. As the Saudis probably anticipated, the Israeli government dismissed the initiative. Nevertheless, the fact that the Saudis would launch it in the first place spoke to the regard—even if purely symbolic—in which states of the region held the conflict and were willing to bow to public opinion when it came to Palestinian rights.

Whatever significance Arab governments might have given to the conflict in the past, however, a number of them, led by the Saudi Arabian government, have put the conflict on the back burner of their foreign-policy concerns—if they have not dismissed it altogether. In the true spirit of "the enemy of my enemy is my friend," shared antipathy to Iran brings Israel, Saudi Arabia, and the members of the Saudi-led "anti-terrorism" (i.e., anti-Iran) alliance together in common cause.

In April 2018, Crown Prince Muhammad bin Salman told an interviewer that he believed "Israelis have the right to have their own land."[11] In October of that same year, Israeli prime minister Benjamin Netanyahu paid an official visit to Sultan Qaboos of Oman. Four months later, he shared a platform with the foreign ministers of Saudi Arabia, the UAE, Bahrain, Yemen, and Oman at the Warsaw Summit, originally called by the United States to address "Iran's influence and terrorism in the region."[12] Then the drips turned into a torrent.

Over the course of 2020, the UAE, Bahrain, Sudan, and Morocco normalized relations with Israel in what has come to be called the "Abraham Accords," the high point of the Trump administration's foray into the Middle East. While touted as a masterstroke of diplomacy, the price exacted by each Arab state was high. The UAE, which was not even a sovereign state when Israel was founded or began its occupation of the West Bank, was promised F-35s, which the United States had been reluctant to sell them; Bahrain got a free-trade agreement with the United States; Sudan got cash and was removed from the list of state sponsors of terrorism; and Morocco got recognition of its claims to Western Sahara.

Even had there been no quid pro quo, however, the "masterstroke of diplomacy" was hardly so. In fact, it was totally retrograde. Although from 1948 to 1993 most of the world viewed the conflict as one between Israel and various Arab states, in reality the conflict concerns—and has always concerned—Israel and the Palestinians, the people dispossessed by the founding of Israel. Israel itself recognized this when it signed on to the Oslo Accord in 1993 and began direct negotiations with representatives of the Palestinian national movement. To put it in legal terms, none of the Arab states that signed on to the normalization agreements has standing. The agreements thus do nothing to bring the conflict closer to resolution. The only ones who can do that are Israelis and Palestinians.

Contrary to the beliefs of those who view the agreements as some sort of breakthrough, the attempt to take the Palestinian issue off the table is a symptom of a disease, not its cure. That disease is a dangerous polarization in the Middle East at a time when conventional diplomatic avenues for crisis management are lacking and threat inflation is commonplace among adversaries.

# 5

# HUMAN SECURITY IN THE NEW MIDDLE EAST

## What is "human security"?

When the term "security" is used among policymakers and political scientists, more often than not it refers to the security of states, not the security of those who live within them. The term "human security" was therefore invented to shift the focus to those factors that make populations unsafe as the first step to rendering them less so. According to the United Nations Development Programme (UNDP), human security is "the liberation of human beings from those intense, extensive, prolonged, and comprehensive threats to which their lives and freedom are vulnerable."[1]

In 2009, the UNDP published *The Arab Human Development Report: Challenges to Human Security in the Arab Countries*. The report lists seven "dimensions" of the threat to human security in the Arab world: "people and their insecure environment"; "the state and its insecure people"; "the vulnerability of those lost from sight"; "volatile growth, high unemployment and persisting poverty"; "hunger, malnutrition and food insecurity"; "health security challenges"; and "occupation and military intervention." Needless to say, the Arab world and, indeed, the entirety of the Middle East are regions in which the threats to human security are among the greatest in the world.

There are problems, however, with measuring human security in the Middle East as a whole. First off, the non-GCC Arab world currently tends to be more vulnerable to certain types of threats to human security than its non-Arab and oil-exporting Arab neighbors. Among them are political instability and the breakdown of states, proxy wars and foreign interventions, the spread of sectarianism, huge increases in refugee flows, economic stagnation, an insecure food supply, and the inability of states to adapt successfully to the neo-liberal blueprint or to take advantage of globalization (with the exception of sub-Saharan Africa, the Arab region outside the Gulf is the least globalized region in the world). While non-Arab-majority and GCC states in the region have their own vulnerabilities, those facing the non-GCC Arab world are on a whole different level of magnitude.

Even within states different groups experience differing levels of human security. Shi'is in Saudi Arabia and Lebanon, the Amazigh (Berber) population of Morocco, the stateless rural minority in Kuwait known as *bidoons* (withouts), guest workers in the GCC countries who make up 70 percent of the employed population, and the 20 percent of Israelis who are of Palestinian descent fare worse in terms of human security in comparison with those among whom they live. Infant mortality for Israelis of Palestinian descent is twice as high as that of Jewish Israelis, while the former can expect to live three to four years less than the latter.

Whatever the drawbacks in using the totality of the Middle East as a unit of analysis, however, it is important to note that many of the greatest threats to human security affect populations throughout the region, Arab and non-Arab alike. Among those threats are poverty, global warming, environmental degradation, haphazard urbanization, and desertification.

## How do population pressures affect the Middle East?

There were approximately 538 million people living in the Middle East in 2021—up from 230 million in 1980. Although the rate of growth is declining in the region, the more than doubling of the population in a little over forty years has strained available resources and state capacities.

Two factors in particular have added to that strain. First, in the Arab world there is the youth bulge. Just as the millennials—those born between the early 1980s and the late 1990s/early 2000s in the United States—make up the largest generational cohort in American history, their equivalent in the Arab world—those roughly between the ages of ten and twenty-four—is also the largest. As of 2022, approximately one-third of all Arabs in the Middle East and North Africa were between those ages.

In both the case of the millennials and the Arab world's youth bulge, the reason for their numbers is the same: These are the children of baby boomers. In the case of the United States, the baby boom is associated with the return of the GIs from World War II and the prosperity of the 1950s and 1960s. In the Arab world, the baby boom came a bit later, when the interventionist states that emerged during the Period of Decolonization began leaving their mark. The interventionist state brought with it improvements in education, public health, and sanitation. Infant mortality declined, as did the numbers of women who died in childbirth. But there is a downside as well: While being part of a large cohort increased competition among millennials for jobs, housing, services, and the like in the United States, their Arab counterparts have faced even greater challenges as a result of slow economic growth and lower levels of prosperity.

The second factor that has strained resources in the Middle East is urbanization. In 1970, about 42 percent of the inhabitants of the Middle East as a whole lived in urban areas. By 2020, more than 65 percent did. The Middle East today is the second-most-urbanized region in the world (Latin America is the first). And the region not only includes large urban concentrations, but megacities—cities with over ten million inhabitants—as well. For example, Cairo, with over twenty million inhabitants, ranked as the seventh largest city in the world in 2022. Overcrowding and the strain that puts on infrastructure and services are reasons the Egyptian government gave in 2015 when it announced a plan to construct a whole new capital city about thirty miles east of the current one. (It should come as no surprise that there is no place for the equivalent of a Tahrir Square in the new capital.) Istanbul (#13, with a population close to sixteen million in 2022) and Tehran (#38, more than nine million) share the same problems as Cairo.

Urban growth in the region exceeded total population growth. This indicates that a major factor in this growth has been rural-to-urban migration. The flight of 1.5 million Syrians from the countryside to provincial cities and major urban areas between 2006 and 2010 is just one example of how the push of rural poverty, even without the pull of urban opportunity, has affected the region. The influx of impoverished rural populations into cities throughout the region (the exception here being Israel) has led to what Egyptian sociologist Saad Eddin Ibrahim has called "urbanization without urbanism."[2] For Ibrahim, the "qualitative change in people's outlook, behavioral patterns, and the organizational networks which they create and participate in" is not taking place in the Middle East as a result of urbanization. The result is the expansion of cities devoid of a binding civic culture.

### What are the effects of diminishing water supplies on the Middle East?

Although agriculture was invented in the Middle East, the region comprises one of the harshest environments on earth. It is certainly one of the most arid. And that aridity is growing. Increases in population have led to overgrazing, unregulated land use, and soil exhaustion. These, in turn, have led to expanding areas of desert (desertification). According to the Arab Centre for the Study of Arid Zones and Dry Lands, desertification threatens almost half the land area in Arab southwest Asia, 30 percent in the Nile Valley and Horn of Africa, 17 percent in North Africa, and 9 percent in the Arabian Peninsula.

Populations have already felt the effects of expanding swaths of parched territory, along with drought and the near exhaustion of reserves of fresh water. Hydrologists—scientists who study water and its flow—measure something they call "water stress" of areas or countries. What they mean by this is the demand for water compared to its availability. According to hydrologists, seventeen countries globally are currently experiencing, on average, "extremely high baseline" levels of water stress; that is, populations currently withdraw more than 80 percent of available water annually for agriculture, industry, and municipalities. Of the seventeen, eleven (Qatar, Israel, Lebanon, Iran, Jordan, Libya, Kuwait, Saudi Arabia, UAE, Bahrain, and Oman, in order) are located in the Middle East. Another eight (Yemen, Morocco, Algeria, Tunisia, Syria, Turkey, Iraq, Egypt) are experiencing "high baseline" levels; that is, populations withdraw more than 40 percent.

To put it another way, according to hydrologists, three Arab countries out of twenty-two were below the water poverty line in 1955. People living in those countries had fewer than fifty liters of water a day—the bare necessity—for drinking, personal hygiene, bathing, and laundry needs. By 1990 there were eleven. By 2025, hydrologists predict that this number will reach eighteen.

Scientists and social scientists disagree on how increasing drought and desertification will affect political stability in the region. Some have pointed to the timing of drought in Syria's northeastern breadbasket—2006–2010—and the outbreak of the Syrian uprising in 2011, which occurred in tandem. The drought, which meteorologists claim was the worst in either five hundred or nine hundred years, turned 60 percent of the country into desert and resulted in the deaths or slaughter of 80 percent of Syrian livestock. It also resulted in a rural-to-urban migratory wave. This is the link most commonly used to connect the drought with a disaffected urban underclass primed for rebellion, and with the rebellion itself.

A tidy theory—but one that some environmental scholars call "anecdotal" and "coincidental."[3] It ignores other causes for Syrian agricultural collapse (such as poor agricultural practices and neo-liberal-inspired removal of fuel subsidies for farmers) and the cyclical nature of Syrian droughts. It also ignores the rapid recovery of Syrian agriculture after 2010 and the reappearance of severe drought in 2021 at a time when the worst of Syria's violence was diminishing. Most of all, it denies agency to Syrians who decided in 2011 that enough was enough and took to the streets. The moral of the story is that in the future, climate will determine possibilities, not outcomes.

But even if the link between water supply and insurrection within a country *is* merely anecdotal and coincidental, the link between water supply and interstate conflict is undeniable.

Only 43 percent of surface water in the Middle East originates within a single country. This has led to conflict and threats of conflict between states over water rights. For example, in 2011 Ethiopia laid the cornerstone for the Grand Ethiopian Renaissance Dam on the Blue Nile, a tributary of the Nile River. The project, which hearkens back to the colossal infrastructural projects so dear to developmental experts during the early post–World War II period, is expected to provide hydroelectric power to expand electrical production for use in Ethiopia and for sale to Ethiopia's neighbors.

But Ethiopia's downstream neighbor, Egypt, is bitterly opposed to the project. Egyptians fear that it will permanently diminish *their* share of the Nile's waters, vital for Egyptian agriculture. In 2013 the Muslim Brotherhood president of Egypt was even caught discussing creative methods to destroy the dam in a meeting with Egyptian politicians. (Unbeknownst to them, the conversation was televised.) While cooler heads prevailed—and the president was removed anyway in a coup d'état—the dam remained such a flashpoint that multiple outsiders have taken a stab at mediating the dispute. These have included the US Treasury, the World Bank, the UAE, and the African Union. In the meantime, Ethiopia continued to fill the dam's reservoir, and Egypt continued to rattle its saber.

The Egyptian-Ethiopian row was not an isolated incident. Similar conflicts have pitted Turkey against Syria and Iraq, and Israel against its neighbors. The former case also involved the construction of a dam, this time built on the headwaters of the Euphrates River, which runs through all three countries. The dam's opening in 1990 goaded Syria into funding the PKK in retaliation. In 1964, Israel's unilateral decision to divert what it claimed was its fair share of water from the Jordan River led to a military confrontation with Syria. That confrontation was the first step down a path that eventually led to the 1967 war between Israel and its Arab neighbors. As a matter of fact, Israel considered its access to water from the Jordan River of such vital concern that capturing the Golan watershed shaped its strategy on the Syrian front during the war. It also makes relinquishing that annexed territory improbable.

The struggle over water also bedevils relations between Israelis and Palestinians. In 1995, the two sides signed an agreement which divided water from the so-called Mountain Aquifer in the West Bank between them. The aquifer supplies almost all of the water used in the West Bank and about one-third of that used in Israel. According to the agreement, Israel was to get 80 percent, the Palestinians the rest. The agreement was to have been revisited in 1999. It wasn't. But as of 2022, Israel had taken 86 percent of the waters, and the Palestinians got the remainder.

In addition to a lack of water to go around in the region, there is, increasingly, a lack of sufficient supplies of clean water. Poor and unregulated public health practices are partly to blame. For example, according to the UN Environment's Fresh Water Unit, upstream communities in Iraq pumped close to 6.7 million cubic yards of raw sewage water *daily* into the Tigris River in 2019. Other reasons for the lack of clean water in the region include runoff of chemical fertilizers and pesticides, salinization, and the venality and corruption of governments that allow Europe to use their states as trash receptacles for its waste, much of which is toxic.

### What is the impact of war on the environment in the Middle East?

While most analysts of World War I have concentrated on the political, diplomatic, social, and even cultural effects of the war, the great Soviet geochemist Vladimir Vernadsky (1863–1945) took a decidedly different route. Vernadsky viewed the war as a great geologic event that resulted in, among other things, the accumulation of huge amounts of lead in the soil of battlefields. That lead affected soil fertility, grazing, and water quality. War, in other words, not only takes a human toll, it takes an environmental one as well. And since the Middle East has been the site of more than its fair share of wars, it only stands to reason that war's environmental impact there has been of enormous consequence.

When it comes to war-induced environmental catastrophes, Iraq probably sets the standard. When Saddam Hussein's forces were fleeing Kuwait in 1991, they set upward of 700 oil rigs on fire, prompting talk of climate change caused by smoke blocking out the sun. In addition, there were deliberate and accidental oil spills. Before and during the war, between twenty-five and fifty million barrels of unburned oil flowed from damaged facilities, temporarily making the Persian Gulf an environmental disaster area. Media critics have argued that images of oil-soaked waterfowl on American television were instrumental in mobilizing domestic support in the United States for the war. After the war, Saddam drained the 6,000 square miles of marshland in southern Iraq. He did so to expose Shi'is who fled there after he had put down their rebellion, along with the indigenous (Shi'i) Marsh Arabs, to his wrath. By the time the United States invaded Iraq in 2003, only 7 percent of the marshland remained.

Over the years, much of the marshlands has recovered. But twenty-five years after their near destruction, Iraq became the site of another environmental calamity in the making: the potential collapse of the Mosul Dam as a result of faulty construction and neglect—or even deliberate sabotage. The fear that ISIS would capture the dam and unleash the waters on downriver populations was one of the reasons the Obama administration gave for the American campaign against the group. At the time, it was estimated that should the dam fail, upward of 1.5 million Iraqis might drown in what the American embassy in Iraq called an "inland tidal wave."[4]

Yemen provides another illustration of the relationship between armed conflict and environmental degradation. While war between government forces and their allies, on the one hand, and Houthi rebels and theirs, on the other, has ground on since 2014, Yemenis and their lived environment have paid a steep price. Outside the capital Sana, a 1,870-ton mountain of garbage has piled up, rotting in the sun. The pile includes waste from Sana's hospitals, haphazardly tossed away since the Saudis destroyed the medical waste incinerator in an airstrike in 2015. In the meantime, fuel cutoffs have compelled the city's 722 bakeries to rely on illegally obtained firewood to bake their bread. This has resulted in the deforestation of 82 square miles of surrounding wooded area and its erosion and desertification. Farther along the coast, the destruction of pipelines by Houthi insurgents cut off clean water supplies for millions and contributed to the spread of a reported 2.5 million cases of cholera.

A further environmental threat posed by the Yemen conflict looms off the Red Sea coast, where a decaying floating storage and off-loading (FSO) tanker filled with more than a million barrels of oil threatens to break apart and spill its contents.

This would destroy fisheries and disrupt passage through the Bab al-Mandeb waterway. Fighting and a blockade that began in 2015 prevented the salvaging of the vessel. Although both the government and the insurgents eventually agreed to a UN plan to avert disaster, the organization initially lacked the financial resources to undertake it. Like a local charity, it had to resort to crowdsourcing to raise money. UN salvage operations began in spring 2023.

### How might climate change affect the Middle East?

In summer 2022, heat buckled railroad tracks in the United Kingdom, and overburdened electric companies in California imposed rolling blackouts on their subscribers. Around the same time, *Reviews of Geophysics* published an article titled "Climate Change and Weather Extremes in the Eastern Mediterranean and Middle East."[5] According to the authors of the article, the region was warming at twice the rate of the rest of the globe, with temperatures rising 9°F by the end of the twenty-first century. The article also predicted droughts of increasing frequency and intensity, marine heat waves, a regional sea level rise, wildfires, and more frequent sandstorms. There is no doubt, the report added, that climate change is "anthropogenic"—man-made. "The human influence on the Earth's climate, including atmospheric, ocean and land components, is unequivocal," it states, adding that the Middle East has overtaken the EU and India as a "dominant emitter" of greenhouse gases.

This was not the first time alarm bells sounded about global warming in the region. During summer 2016 the Middle East reached a new milestone: Temperatures in Kuwait rose to the highest point ever recorded on the planet outside Death Valley, California—129.2°F. Kuwait did not broil alone. Temperatures reached 126°F in Iran and Iraq. In fact, the Middle East as a whole was scorching. While scientists were once divided about whether the extremely high temperatures were an aberration or will become the new normal, most now agree that unless climate-warming greenhouse gases are reduced, there will be no turning back. They forecast that Doha, Qatar; Abu Dhabi in the United Arab Emirates; and Bandar Abbas, Iran will soon reach a felt temperature (combined heat and humidity) of 170°F—the temperature at which human habitation becomes impossible.

Although climate change will affect every region of the globe, the Middle East is more vulnerable than most for two reasons. The first has to do with food.

Because of difficult agricultural conditions throughout the Middle East, the region imports more food, particularly grains, than does any other region in the world. Fifty percent of Egyptian food and 97 percent of its wheat, for example, come from abroad, mostly from Russia (61 percent) and Ukraine (24 percent)—which is one reason why the war in Ukraine, which severely limited exports from that country, was so devastating to Egypt's economy. In 2010—the year before the Egyptian uprising—wild fires and a heat wave diminished the Russian crop by 40 percent, and Russia took its grain off the international market. Over the course of the following year, food prices in Egypt jumped 30 percent. Scientists have attributed the wild fires and heat wave to climate change.

The second reason that the Middle East is vulnerable to climate change is that a large proportion of the region's population lives in coastal areas. According to the World Bank, there are currently forty-three heavily inhabited coastal areas in the region, from Casablanca, Morocco, in the west to Bandar Abbas in the east. As temperatures rise and polar ice caps shrink, sea levels rise. Predictions about the effects of rising sea levels on coastal populations are dire: Scientists estimate that a temperature increase of 2° to 5°F would expose six to twenty-five million North Africans to coastal flooding. A half-meter rise in sea levels would displace more than two million inhabitants of Alexandria alone. Rising sea levels would also lead to the further salinization of fresh water sources. Populations that depend on coastal aquifers, such as the population of Gaza, are particularly vulnerable. More than two million inhabitants of the territory depend on a single aquifer, which they share with Israel.

### What is the refugee crisis all about?

Before the current refugee crisis, the largest group of refugees in the Middle East was made up of Palestinians who had been displaced during the 1948 and 1967 wars, along with their descendants (although the Trump administration sought to strip the descendants of those who fled of their refugee status, the Biden administration simply ignored the switch). There are approximately 5.6 million Palestinian refugees currently registered with the United Nations High Commissioner for Refugees (UNHCR). Many others are nonregistered. Among them are those who have been able to escape life in the refugee camps because they could afford to or because they were able to emigrate abroad. While the rights of Palestinians vary from country to country, Jordan is the only country in the Arab world that has offered Palestinian refugees full rights of citizenship (the Jordanian population is divided between those who lived there before 1948 and their descendants—known as "East Bankers"—and Palestinians, who make up a majority of the population).

Now, of course, the attention of the world has shifted to Syrian refugees, particularly those who have sought asylum outside the region. Commentators use the term "refugees" to refer to the Syrians who have left their homes and emigrated abroad deliberately. They differentiate between migrants and refugees. For them, migrants are those who leave their country of origin for economic reasons. Refugees, they maintain, leave for political reasons or because they are fleeing a war zone. In fact, no clear differentiation can be made. Political turbulence frequently leaves economic deprivation in its wake.

Furthermore, those who flee one country for political reasons might decamp from their new home for economic ones.

About one million refugees sought asylum in Europe in 2015, and more than 100,000 during the first three months of 2016. This marked the peak of what has been termed in the West the "refugee crisis." Most of these refugees came from countries that surround Syria. The reason for the surge in emigration to Europe was that the Syrian civil war had dragged on for years. Many of those who had thought of the camps as a temporary refuge simply gave up hope of ever returning to their homes. Others left to escape deepening poverty or an inability to obtain work permits in the countries where they had sought refuge. Still others left because of the lack of educational opportunities for themselves or their children, or because aid shortfalls made their lives in the camps unbearable.

Donald Trump made "Muslim refugees" a campaign issue in 2016, and when he was president he issued three versions of an executive order banning mostly Muslim travelers from entering the United States. Those who promoted the bans played to the fears of a public unaware of the true nature of the refugee population. According to statistics gathered by the UNCHR in May 2016, the refugee population was nearly evenly split between men and women. Only about 22 percent were men between the ages of eighteen and fifty-nine—the gender and age range many Americans associate with terrorists. About 56 percent were under the age of seventeen—and 39 percent of those were under eleven. A sampling of refugees in Greece shows that a large number of adults—86 percent—had secondary or university education. Most of them were under thirty-five. Syria is thus losing the very people it will most need if there is to be any hope of rebuilding in the future.

In March 2016 the European Union reached an agreement with Turkey setting the rules for refugees wishing to emigrate from Turkey to Europe. According to the plan, Greece was to return to Turkey all "new irregular migrants" (those not cleared first in camps in Turkey) traveling from Turkey to the

Greek islands, where many land. In return, the member states of the European Union promised to allow an equal number of Syrian refugees residing in Turkey to emigrate to Europe. They also promised to boost existing financial support for the refugees still in Turkey. To make the deal even more palatable for the Turks, they agreed to make it easier for Turkish nationals to obtain visas for Europe.

International refugee and rights organizations were up in arms. Not only was the agreement inhumane, they argued, it violated European Union and international standards regarding refugees. According to those standards, states could not detain refugees involuntarily and refugees had the right to appeal their deportation. Nevertheless, the agreement remained in effect.

In addition to a refugee crisis, the Middle East has a related crisis on its hands: The region harbors an unusually high number of internally displaced persons (IDPs), both in Syria and elsewhere. IDPs are people who have left their homes but have not crossed an international border. The Middle East has more IDPs than does any other region in the world. This is, in large measure, the result of the lawlessness that has accompanied state breakdown and the violence of civil wars and foreign interventions (such as the American invasion and occupation of Iraq and the Saudi intervention into Yemen's civil war).

As of 2020, there were 6.9 million IDPs in Syria, 4.3 million in Yemen, upward of 3.76 million in Turkey (many as a result of the Kurdish insurgency and the government's counterinsurgency campaign), 1.2 million in Iraq, 280,000 in Libya, and 263,500 in the Palestinian territories (displaced from 1948 through 2014). These numbers wax as conflicts escalate, authorities discourage return, or safety remains a concern for the displaced. They wane as struggles de-escalate, authorities assure safe passage, or conflicts grind on without an end in sight, emboldening restless IDPs to return to their homes.

IDPs have an advantage over refugees because they enjoy the rights of citizenship in their new homes. On the other hand, IDPs frequently lack access to schooling, healthcare, family networks, and employment opportunities. They also suffer disproportionately from depression and post-traumatic stress disorder. And during the COVID-19 pandemic, displaced populations suffered from higher rates of infection as well as economic disruption caused by lockdowns and business closures.

### What is the status of women in the Middle East?

The 2005 Arab Human Development Report, titled "Towards the Rise of Women in the Arab World," begins as follows:

Compared to their sisters elsewhere in the world, [Arab women] enjoy the least political participation. Conservative authorities, discriminatory laws, chauvinist male peers and tradition-minded kinsfolk watchfully regulate their aspirations, activities and conduct. Employers limit their access to income and independence. In the majority of cases, poverty shackles the development and use of women's potential. High rates of illiteracy and the world's lowest rates of female labour participation are compounded to "create serious challenges." Though a growing number of individual women, supported by men, have succeeded in achieving greater equality in society and more reciprocity in their family and person relationships, many remain victims of legalized discrimination, social subordination, and enshrined male dominance.[6]

How has the Arab world fared since the report was written? Every year, the World Economic Forum publishes its *Gender Gap Report*, which ranks regions and countries on the basis of such variables as women's economic participation, their educational attainment, their health and survival, and their political empowerment. Overall, in 2020 the MENA region (which includes Israel, Turkey, and Iran as well as the Arab world) did not fare very well. As a matter of fact, aside from Israel (#64), the rankings of the countries of the region were dismal, ranging from the UAE (#120) and Kuwait (#122) to Iraq (#152) and Yemen (#153—dead last globally). Even Tunisia, whose post-uprising constitution boldly declared that men and women "have equal rights and duties and are equal before the law without any discrimination" could do no better than #124 globally. (Adding insult to injury, a 2024 electoral law stripped women of the right to gender parity regardless of constitutional guarantees.)

Overall, of the bottom ten countries of the world, seven were in the region. While the health and educational gender gaps between men and women were narrow, the political power and economic gaps were yawning.

Of course, the status and condition of women in the Arab world differ in significant ways from country to country. While women in Rojava continue to enjoy parity in all elected assemblies, the requirement in Egypt that voters must show their ID's effectively suppresses the votes of women, who are less likely to have one. In 2019, the prime minister of the UAE decreed equal pay for men and women for equal work; in Egypt's private sector, women's wages are 80 percent lower than men's. Jordan boasts of a literacy rate of about 98 percent for women; in Iraq, it is 44 percent. In spite of the variations, however, the truth remains: statistically speaking, as of 2020 the MENA region was the worst region in the world to be a woman.

The subordination of women in the Middle East has played out in a number of ways, from violence against them and child marriage (which, however, is declining) to honor killings (the murder of a female family member for purportedly bringing shame on the family) and female genital mutilation (or

FGM—the removal of external female genitalia). Performed to control women's sexuality, FGM is widespread in a number of countries. In 2022, for example, UNICEF estimated that 87.2 percent of Egyptian women between the ages of fifteen and forty-nine had undergone the "procedure." (That only 18.5 percent of Yemeni women in the same age range experienced it demonstrates that FGM is a subregional custom, not an Islamic or Arab one.)

Female subordination manifests itself in other ways as well. Although women in all countries in the Middle East have the right to vote (Saudi Arabia, the last on board, bowed to the inevitable in 2011), voting in most of the region is not exactly empowering. Women still lag in participation in governance at the highest levels behind their sisters in every other region of the world (Israel and Rojava being exceptions). And in terms of family issues, most Middle Eastern women are trapped in an entrenched patriarchy. According to a 2013 Pew Research Center Poll, on average 86 percent of Arabs polled (male and female) believed that a wife must always obey her husband, 63 percent believed family planning was not morally acceptable, and 35 percent believed polygamy morally acceptable. Only 38 percent believed a woman should have the right to divorce her husband and only 26 percent believed that daughters should have inheritance rights equal to that of sons.[7]

Most international development agencies agree that economic development hinges on women's participation in the labor force. Unfortunately, overall female participation in the Arab workforce was about 18 percent in 2021—among the lowest in the world. Of course, this number varies from country to country, with the lowest participation in war-torn Yemen and Iraq— 6 percent and 11 percent, respectively. That same year, it was 47 percent in Kuwait, 55 percent in the UAE and 57 percent in Qatar—just two percentage points below Israel. In addition to entrenched cultural biases against hiring women, women lack employment opportunities in the Arab world because of high reproductive rates, legal systems that make hiring women difficult, and personal status regulations. For example, in some places women need their father's or husband's permission to work. Low female employment means that dependency ratios—the number of dependents each worker supports—are the highest in the world, increasing the numbers of those who live in poverty.

Lack of educational opportunities also hinders women's participation in the workforce. The Arab world has one of the world's lowest rates of female education (above only sub-Saharan Africa) and, again along with sub-Saharan Africa, the largest gap between male and female education. On the other hand, when women do have access to post-secondary education, they take advantage of it. As of 2020 there were more women than men attending universities in ten Arab countries for which data is available (as well as in Israel and Iran). Of these, 34–57 percent are studying STEM (45 percent of American women at US universities are studying STEM).

The outlook for women in the Middle East is thus not uniformly bleak, and governments throughout the region have pushed back against women's subordination, with varying degrees of commitment and success. There are three reasons for the pushback. First, it has been in their interest to do so. Secular-minded rulers from Morocco to pre-revolutionary Iran have for years advocated for women as part of their development strategy. They have also used the issue to expand their base of support—and diminish support for oppositional Islamist movements—by reaching out to women and to male liberals. And it did not hurt that their campaigns on behalf of women demonstrated to the outside world the great strides their countries were making and how enlightened their leadership was. Thus, the last shah of Iran appointed his sister honorary head of the High Council of Iranian Women's Associations, and local media dubbed laws expanding women's personal rights in Egypt "Jehan's laws" and "Suzanne's laws" after the presidential wives who purportedly promoted them.

In addition, the logic of neo-liberalism demands a broadening of the marketplace to include the full range of producers and consumers. It is no coincidence that the IMF strongly supports female participation in the labor force, as do all the "Vision" plans of the GCC states, which highlight the role women will play in the new national economies. Goal #5 of Kuwait's "Vision 2035," for example, pledges to "achieve gender equality and empower all women and girls" to "create human capital" for the market.[8]

In addition to the logic of neo-liberalism, there is another logic at play. Some of the most autocratic leaders in modern times have supported women's rights. This is not because they felt a sudden urge to spread the range of civil liberties available to their populations. That would have been too out of character. Instead, they have supported women's rights because they have sought to expand the reach of the state into the home, and to replace the "private patriarchy" of the husband/father-dominated family with a "public patriarchy" defined by the state. There has been no shortage of autocrats who have used this strategy in the Middle East.

All three reasons for spurning facets of women's subordination are at play in Saudi Arabia, where Crown Prince Muhammad bin Salman has found expanding women's rights and opportunities useful for achieving his personal political ambitions as well as his economic ones. Women's workforce participation in 2018 was 20 percent; in 2021, nearly 34 percent. The government has at long last granted women the right to drive—although Loujain al-Hathloul, who led the campaign for that right, remained in prison even after that right was granted, and a woman's guardian must still grant her permission to sit behind the wheel. The government has also granted women the right to mix with men in some public spaces like coffee shops, attend sporting events, and apply for passports and travel abroad without permission from their male guardian. The crown prince also clipped the wings of the religious police, which no longer enforces public morality.

It is hardly coincidental that these changes have taken place at a time when the crown prince has been consolidating power and expanding his control over the government. They certainly don't demonstrate a budding feminist sensibility in someone whose crimes and overstepping made him an international pariah. In addition to fostering the necessary backdrop to realize "Vision 2030," loosening restrictions on women and curtailing some aspects of the guardianship system expands the reach of the state into the most personal of realms—the family. In other words, it replaces a private patriarchal system with a public one.

### To what extent was the COVID-19 pandemic a game changer?

Doctors reported the first cases of COVID-19 in the Middle East in the UAE at the end of January 2020. The patients were four members of a family that had traveled to Dubai from Wuhan, China, the global epicenter of the disease. At the time of their diagnosis, the COVID-19 virus had killed 132 people, mostly in China.

As it did elsewhere, the disease spread quickly in the Arab world. According to reports, by June 2022, the virus had infected 13 million people and killed about 170,000. Its spread was uneven, ranging from 380 officially reported cases per million people in Yemen to 324,000 in Bahrain (this statistic undoubtedly attests to the difficulty of collecting data in Yemen, and, if accurate, to its isolation from global commerce).

As the case of Yemen indicates, reliable data about COVID-19 infections and deaths in the Middle East are hard to come by. Take the case of Egypt. The Sisi regime viewed the spread of COVID-19 there as much as a public relations problem as a public health one. The regime went so far as to ship crucial medical supplies to China, Italy, and the United States to bolster its image abroad. (The regime also used the spread of COVID-19 as an excuse to expand repression, censorship, and surveillance—tools which came naturally to it—but that is another story.) According to the government sources, by spring 2022 the death toll in Egypt from COVID-19 had reached close to twenty-five thousand. According to the World Health Organization, the real number was closer to 280,000.

The effectiveness of government response in the region was uneven. The wealthy GCC states had more advanced medical systems and resources. This enabled them to test, prevent viral spread, and cushion the economic damage caused by the pandemic (in July 2021, the magazine *Global Finance* ranked the UAE and Qatar the second and third safest countries in the world in terms of COVID-19, outranked only by Iceland). Other MENA states were not so fortunate. Years of neo-liberal economic policies and disinvestment in medical infrastructure stretched public health resources beyond their capacity. Local conditions also took a toll: it is estimated that 70 percent of Syrian healthcare workers left the country during the conflict there, and the Syrian army and Russian air force deliberately targeted medical facilities and personnel. To the west, the port explosion in Beirut destroyed half of the city's medical care facilities. Beirut is home to about 30 percent of the Lebanese population.

Outside the Arab world, both Iran and Turkey were hard hit. The Iranian government blamed US sanctions, but government corruption was likely to blame as well. In the case of Turkey, the culprit was probably a government that placed economic over public health considerations.

As the COVID-19 crisis began to shift from pandemic to endemic status—that is, as the coronavirus became more of a seasonal fact of life like the flu and less of a mortal threat— international organizations and aid agencies, as well as think tanks, tried to assess the damage left behind. They found higher levels of income poverty and unemployment, greater income inequality (both inside states and across boundaries), diminished quality and access to healthcare and education, and lower levels of trust in governing institutions, among other things, scattered throughout the Middle East region.

And throughout the region COVID-19-related restrictions on movement and public activity expanded governments' ability to control and surveil their populations wherever they were put in place.

What remains to be seen is the sticking power of these COVID-19-induced effects. COVID-19 may have shifted the landscape in the Middle East long-term, much as the demographic boom and the neo-liberal revolution had done previously. Or its effects may prove to be a temporary aberration and the region may shortly return to business as usual. Think of how the jolt of 9/11 was supposed to change American culture forever—but did not. Most likely is the possibility that we shall witness something between long-term disruption and insignificant blip.

### How poor is the Middle East?

In terms of human security, a number of trends were discernible in the New Middle East before the advent of COVID-19. Those trends will likely provide the benchmarks for the region as it emerges from the pandemic. Among those benchmarks was the incidence of poverty.

Development experts differentiate between "income poverty" and "human poverty." Income poverty focuses on a single variable—the amount of money an individual or household has at its disposal. Human poverty is a more encompassing metric that not only includes income, but takes quality-of-life factors into account as well.

Income poverty is measured in two ways. The first quantifies the number of people living in "extreme poverty." Those who live in extreme poverty have less than $1.90 per day—the international standard—available for expenditures. According to this measure, the Middle East's record has been mixed. Those living in extreme poverty in the predominantly Arab part of the Middle East numbered 170 million in 1993 (until 2015, extreme poverty was defined as an income of less than

$1.25 per day). That number declined until it reached 107 million in 2010. It then began to climb again, mainly as a result of political instability and conflict. The distribution of those living in extreme poverty is thus unevenly spread across the region. In 2015, 21 percent of Iraqis and 37 percent of Yemenis lived in extreme poverty. On the other hand, the number of citizens of Qatar and the UAE who lived in extreme poverty that year—if there were any—was negligible.

The $1.90 per capita per day measure is not the only way statisticians calculate income poverty. They also go by a country's poverty line, which each country determines for itself based on local conditions. This measure of income poverty is more expansive than the first because it measures all those who live below the national poverty line, not just those who live in extreme poverty.

According to this measure, income poverty in much of the Middle East has been on the rise since the end of the past century. The three main reasons given for the rising numbers of those living below the poverty line in the Middle East are neoliberal policies, which have removed parts of the social safety net; high rates of unemployment; and, most significantly, conflict in the Arab parts of the region.

In 2014, sixteen of the twenty-one states in the region registered unemployment rates higher than the international mean of 9.4 percent (that year only Turkey, Israel, Kuwait, the UAE, and Qatar, in descending order, were below the mean). While there were a number of factors that contributed to those rates, from privatization-induced layoffs to a growth in population that far exceeded the economic growth, one statistic in particular stands out: The Arab world was less industrialized in the first decade of this century than it was in 1970.

Economists cite conflict as the single most important reason that the numbers of those living below the poverty line in the region have spiked since 2010. It has been estimated that as of 2014, 28 percent of Iraqis, 33 percent of Libyans, 38 percent of

Gazans, 54 percent of Yemenis, and more than 85 percent of Syrians lived in poverty.

Conflict does not explain, however, why the numbers of those living below the poverty line have also increased in those countries in the Arab world that were less affected by protracted violence. Once again, economists cite neo-liberal economic policies, high unemployment, and political turmoil as culprits. But they also cite a sporadic dip in oil prices, which eats into export revenue; a decline in tourism; the aftershock of the spike in food prices; and job nationalization and the substitution of expatriate Arab labor by South Asian labor in the Gulf.

In Egypt, the percentage of those living below the poverty line increased one point from 2011 to 2016, reaching 26.3 percent. One percentage point does not seem like much, but it means an increase of upward of one million more Egyptians living in poverty in the aftermath of the uprising there. Even Saudi citizens have been affected by adverse conditions. Sociologists estimate (and estimates are the best that can be had in secretive Saudi Arabia) that in 2015 between 7 and 14 percent of Saudis had at their disposal $17 or less per day; that is, they were living at or below the poverty line. Income inequality was higher in Saudi Arabia than in Argentina or the United States.

Using the second measure for poverty, high levels of income poverty in the Middle East might also be found outside the Arab world. In 2016, 21 percent of Israelis lived below the poverty line. Although poverty in Israel is usually associated with the Arab and ultra-Orthodox Jewish populations (a sizeable number of ultra-Orthodox men, preferring religious study to work, live off stipends, government handouts, and their wives' salaries), there have been increasing numbers of working poor in this category as well. As elsewhere, in Israel neo-liberalism has not been the worker's friend.

It is estimated that 70 percent of Iranians and 40 percent of Turks also lived below the poverty line before the onset of COVID-19. Economists attribute poverty in Iran mainly to population growth and international sanctions, which were lifted after Iran signed on to the nuclear agreement, only to be reimposed by the Trump administration. Steps taken by the Iranian government—which oversaw the so-called resistance economy—didn't help either. To counter the sanctions, the government promoted homegrown production to replace imports. The result was the further enrichment of the wealthy and black marketeers in the private sector, as well as agencies owned by the government in the public sector.

To explain the rising level of poverty in pre-pandemic Turkey, economists point to both a global and domestic economic downturn and the government's pro-natalist (pro-birth) policies. To counteract the problems associated with a rapidly aging population, the Turkish government has encouraged women to bear three or more children. Unfortunately, neither the Turkish government nor the Turkish economy can support the increase in family size. High rates of inflation during and after the pandemic only made matters worse.

### What is the state of human poverty in the non–Gulf Cooperation Council Arab world?

Human poverty is measured by something called a multidimensional poverty index, which bases its rankings on three variables: health (as indicated by child mortality and nutrition), education (as measured by years of schooling and child enrollment), and standard of living (as measured by access to electricity, clean drinking water, adequate plumbing and sanitation, flooring, cooking fuel, and family assets). While parts of the Middle East measure well in terms of the index, before the onset of the pandemic human poverty in non-GCC Arab states remained unchanged or had gotten worse. That trend is likely to continue in the post-pandemic Middle East.

One of the primary metrics used to measure human poverty is life expectancy. Life expectancy varies widely across the region. As of 2019, before COVID-19, life expectancy ranged from highs in Israel (82.62 years for both men and women), Kuwait (80.97) Turkey (78.63), and Jordan (77.87) to lows in Syria (72.67), Iraq (72.42), Egypt (71.82), and Yemen (66.63). Surprisingly, except for the last four countries, life expectancy in the Middle East was actually higher than the global norm of 72.74. As in much of the rest of the world, the leading cause of death in the Middle East was heart disease. Where the region diverged from much of the rest of the world were other leading causes of death, including neonatal complications in Yemen (#3), "collective violence and legal intervention" in Syria (#3), diabetes in Bahrain (#2), and road injuries throughout the region. Bad driving, it seems, is endemic to the Middle East and North Africa.

According to the World Health Organization, the number of deaths from infectious disease fell in the Eastern Mediterranean region between 2000 and 2015—although the rate of decline was slightly slower than the global average during this period. There were exceptions to this trend. These included the reintroduction of polio into Syria (probably brought by foreign fighters) and the spread of Middle East Respiratory Syndrome (or MERS, which is transmitted from camels to humans) in Saudi Arabia. More recently, there has been an explosion of HIV infections in the Arab world. The decline in deaths from contagious disease is the good news. The bad news is that fatalities from non-communicable diseases and injuries are on the increase.

One factor contributing to mortality rates in the Arab world is what the United Nations Development Programme calls "food insecurity." There have been times when food has all but disappeared from market stalls. In 2012, for example, there was a 53 percent shortage of grains, and about 10 percent of Arabs were experiencing food shortages—a number that is bound to increase in the future as poverty, climate change, and the effects of political instability and war spread. Two years later, the World Food Programme announced that the percentage of Iraqis, Palestinians, and Yemenis who were un- dernourished hovered around 30 percent. The Russian inva- sion of Ukraine in 2022 added to the periodic misery. The war temporarily blocked Ukrainian grain shipments to the region and contributed to a spike in prices that surpassed the noto- rious price increases of 2010—the year the uprisings began.

The consequences of political instability and war for nu- trition in the region have been particularly felt in Syria and Yemen. During the 1990s, Syria produced so much food that it could export the surplus. Then came the 2006–2010 drought. After 2011, things got even worse: Following the outbreak of the uprising, the Syrian government began laying siege to urban areas, using starvation as a weapon. In January 2016, the United Nations estimated that 400,000 people in fifteen separate parts of the country were going hungry. In one town alone (Madaya), twenty-three Syrians starved to death in December 2015.

War had a similar effect on Yemen. Before the Saudi inter- vention into the Yemeni civil war, Yemen imported 90 per- cent of the food it needed. Once they entered the war, the Saudis imposed a blockade on Yemeni ports, cutting off food deliveries. As a result, by late summer 2016 the World Food Program classified ten of Yemen's twenty-two provinces as one step away from famine. In the course of a year, the number of Yemeni children at risk from severe acute malnutrition doubled, reaching 320,000.

While most dramatic in Syria and Yemen, the "calorie crisis" in the Arab world can be found in pockets of poverty throughout the region. It is therefore ironic that the region simultaneously suffers from its opposite as well: an obesity epidemic.

The Middle East is the second most obese region in the world (the South Pacific is the first). In 2021, about 70 per- cent of the adult population of Kuwait, Jordan, Saudi Arabia, Libya, Turkey, Egypt, Lebanon, and the UAE were either over- weight (a Body Mass Index—BMI—of 25 or above) or obese (a

BMI of 30 or above). Public health officials point to a number of reasons for the epidemic: the adoption of Western diets, the spread of a different aesthetic (being plump was once a sign of prosperity in the United States, too), and the perpetuation of "traditional roles" and lack of exercise for women. Along with high levels of tobacco use (more men in Jordan smoke—80 percent—than in any other country in the world) and one of the highest incidences of traffic accidents per car anywhere, obesity-linked diseases are the most preventable killers in the Arab world.

The sorry state of healthcare and public health services in Arab countries outside the GCC make matters worse. From the 1950s through the 1960s, healthcare and public health improved throughout the region. Investment in healthcare and public health infrastructure had been minimal before the postcolonial republics set the regional standards for state intervention into society. Improvements were therefore not difficult to make. Over time, however, the quality of both declined because populations grew at faster rates than states' ability to provide for them. The IMF and the neo-liberal doctrines it promoted also constrained states from undertaking large-scale investments, even for the public good.

As a result, healthcare delivery is poor in the Arab world outside the GCC countries. It is inefficient and underfunded, and it lacks skilled personnel. On average, countries in the region spent a little more than 5 percent of their GDP on healthcare in 2019. Compare that to the United Kingdom, which spent 10.15 percent, or the United States, which spent a whopping 16.77 percent (the GCC countries, which have a huge income-to-population ratio, spend proportionately less). And the situation is bound to worsen as populations age. Currently, individuals cover about half of overall healthcare costs by paying out of pocket. This means they have little protection when faced with catastrophic illness or long-term care. It also means that the wealthy receive far better care than those at the middle income level or the poor, those who have no benefits (such as those living in rural areas), and those who do not work for employers legally obliged to provide them with workers' benefits.

## What is education like in the Arab world?

The sorry state of healthcare is not the only or even primary reason for the poor showing of Arab countries on the multidimensional poverty index. That honor goes to education. Developmental economists today view harnessing knowledge and innovation in the same way their forebears viewed harnessing steam power: the essential motor for success in a competitive world economy. They even talk of building "knowledge-based economies," which, they claim, will ensure continuous growth and full employment wherever they take root. The key to building a knowledge-based economy is investment in education, which will cultivate workers with research, management, and professional skills.

The history of education in the Arab world is similar to the history of healthcare in the region. Postcolonial states throughout the Arab world promoted free public education on all levels, not only to fulfill their side of the ruling bargain, but also to meet development goals. And it didn't hurt that schools provided a venue for the state to inculcate values and ideologies. In 1960, the literacy rate for all Egyptian adults stood at 26 percent; by 2017, it was 80 percent (which was still below the 86 percent global rate). Egyptian women make up the bulk—64 percent—of those who cannot read or write. But literacy is only one metric for rating education. And while literacy is a worthwhile goal in its own right, literacy rates hardly shed light on the quality of education as a whole. As with healthcare, education in the non-GCC Arab world fell victim to rising populations and slow economic growth. The two youth bulges since the early postcolonial period were particularly damaging to the delivery of quality education.

Currently, education in the Arab world, from pre-kindergarten through post-secondary, is notoriously inadequate. According to the 2003 Arab Human Development Report,

> [The] curricula taught in Arab countries seem to encourage submission, obedience, subordination and compliance, rather than free critical thinking. In many cases, the contents of these curricula do not stimulate students to criticise political or social axioms. Instead, they smother their independent tendencies and creativity.[9]

All of the GCC "vision" plans include roadmaps for expanding the reach and quality of education. Whether schools there and in the wider Arab world can change remains to be seen. Schools educate not only by *what* they teach, but *how* they teach. In other words, values held in high regard outside the classroom—such as open debate, creativity, and cooperation in democratic societies—are reproduced and practiced in the classroom setting. Autocratic and highly patriarchal societies prize none of those values which, in turn, are the essential building blocks of a knowledge-based economy.

Twenty-first century education in the Arab Middle East is structurally incapable of promoting debate or critical thinking. Rote memorization is encouraged and only memorization and factual recall are tested. Universities other than foreign branch campuses or universities registered elsewhere (such as the American University in Cairo and the American University in Beirut) are under the direct control of the government. They tend to be overcrowded as a result of free tuition, the youth bulge, and neo-liberal budget cutting. They are also staffed by instructors who often are hired and promoted on the basis of political loyalty rather than on the basis of competence. In a number of Arab countries, professors have had to belong to the ruling party. And because they tend to earn meager salaries, they cannot devote themselves fully to teaching and research. The inadequacies of universities in the Arab world are one of the reasons the GCC countries encourage university-age youths to study abroad. It is also one of the reasons those youths are eager to do so. In 2015, 60,000 Saudi students enrolled in American universities alone (the Saudi government changed eligibility requirements in 2019, halving that number). Still, sending students abroad is hardly an adequate way to jump-start knowledge-based economies—particularly since 95 percent of Arab youths who study abroad do not return home.

### Can human security be measured?

In 2000, member states of the United Nations adopted a set of eight "Millennium Development Goals"[10] to be met by the international community during the first fifteen years of the new century. Each goal had enumerated targets. They were as follows:

1. "Eradicate extreme poverty and hunger."
2. "Achieve full and productive employment and decent work for all, including women and young people."
3. "Halve, between 1990 and 2015, the proportion of people who suffer from hunger."
4. "Ensure that by 2015, children everywhere, boys and girls alike, will be able to complete a full course of primary schooling."
5. "Eliminate gender disparity in primary and secondary education, preferably by 2005, and in all levels of education no later than 2015."
6. "Reduce by two thirds, between 1990 and 2015, the under five mortality rate."
7. "Reduce by three quarters between, 1990 and 2015, the maternal mortality ratio."

8. "Achieve, by 2015, universal access to reproductive health."
9. "Have halted and begun to reverse the spread of HIV/ AIDS. Achieve, by 2010, universal access to treatment for HIV/AIDS for all who need it."
10. "Have halted by 2015 and begun to reverse the incidence of malaria and other major diseases."
11. "Integrate the principals of sustainable development into country policies and programs and reverse the loss of environmental resources. Reduce biodiversity loss, achieving, by 2010, a significant reduction in the rate of loss."
12. "Halve, by 2015, the proportion of people without sustainable access to safe drinking water and basic sanitation."
13. "By 2020 to have achieved a significant improvement in the lives of at least 100 million slum dwellers."
14. "Develop further an open, rule-based, predictable, non-discriminatory trading and financial system."
15. "Address the special needs of the least developed countries."
16. "Deal comprehensively with the debt problems of developing countries through national and international measures in order to make debt sustainable in the long term."
17. "In cooperation with the private sector, make available the benefits of new technologies, especially information and communications."

So how did the Arab world do? According to a report published by the UN and the Arab League in 2015, the region posted "a mixed record." The results of the assessment were as follows:

1. "Extreme poverty is low, but has increased dramatically in [the Arab east and least developed countries (LDCs)]." (Of the countries discussed in this book, only Yemen is categorized as an LDC.)

2. "Despite gains in job creation, women's participation in the labour force remains a key challenge."
3. "The region is far behind in meeting the target of halving undernourishment."
4. "Significant gains in primary school enrolment, but LDCs should catch up.
5. "More girls go to school, but the economic and political empowerment of women remains a challenge."
6. "Significant progress in reducing child and infant mortality, but LDCs will not achieve the target."
7. "Maternal mortality is still very high in LDCs."
8. "Access to reproductive healthcare has been improved, but not in LDCs."
9. "The number of people living with HIV is increasing, but more people can now access treatment."
10. "Regional tuberculosis prevalence rates are falling slowly; death rates have declined more substantially."
11. "Carbon dioxide emissions are increasing, while other indicators of environmental sustainability are improving."
12. "Millions more have benefited from access to safe drinking water and basic sanitation, but large subnational disparities remain."
13. "Slums have been virtually eliminated in some Arab countries, while in others conflict has fanned their growth."
14. "The Arab region is still unable to fully utilize the potential of trade liberalization."
15. "Official development assistance to the Arab region is still low and volatile."
16. "Fiscal space for development expenditure in middle-income countries and LDCs is more constrained since 2010."
17. "The Information and Communications Technology (ICT) revolution is spreading in the region."

Overall, the report notes the unevenness within the region of reaching the targets of the Millennium Development Goals. Two other factors undercut the usefulness of the endeavor. First, the fact that Egypt, Syria, Oman, and Tunisia are listed alongside Saudi Arabia as the big winners that "exceeded what is required to meet the MDG targets" is mind-boggling. Syria? Really? In addition, the report was published before crisis states became an enduring feature of the Middle East landscape, multiple new conflict zones opened up, a global pandemic afflicted much of the region, and Russia invaded Ukraine. These factors alone make measuring trends in human security a daunting, if not impossible, task.

### What are the greatest threats to human security in the New Middle East?

Middle Easterners face a myriad of challenges that directly affect human security in the region. Some of these challenges are connected to deep-seated practices.

For example, economists draw a direct link between women's workforce participation and education, on the one hand, and national economic development, on the other. Nevertheless, patriarchal values embedded in the family and political institutions ensure women are disadvantaged in both.

Adult male Yemenis enjoy socializing and chewing qat during their siestas. The leaves of the qat plant contain a stimulant whose affect is somewhat like a double espresso. Yemen, a country in the midst of water and food crises of epic proportions, uses about 40 percent of the water available for agriculture for irrigating its inedible qat crop. (Lest Americans feel smug, it should be noted that during the 2001–2022 California drought—the worst drought in 1,200 years—the state produced 71 percent of America's head lettuce, often used as a garnish for burgers and sandwiches. Lettuce has little caloric value. Waste is in the eyes of the beholder.)

Some threats to human security in the Middle East are less associated with deep-seated social practices. Perhaps the two threats of this sort that loom the largest are what is euphemistically called the "lack of good governance" and the pitiable state of most economies in the region.

The region as a whole measures poorly in terms of corruption, repression, accountability, transparency, democratic practice, respect for the rule of law, and concern for human rights. From Iran's "Green Revolution," which broke out in response to the stolen presidential election of 2009, to the Arab uprisings and social protest movements in Israel (2011) and Turkey (2013), populations took their frustration and anger to the streets. In some places, states responded by warring on them. In others, states lost the ability to ensure public safety. In still others, states called for or opened themselves up to foreign intervention. The result region-wide has been a decrease in human security and a rise in human poverty, both directly and indirectly. In terms of the latter, the uprisings enabled ISIS to gain a foothold in the region and sparked a massive refugee crisis.

The effects of poor governance will continue to spin themselves out in the immediate future. How can regimes that cannot rule effectively or win the support of their populations possibly deal with emerging crises such as those brought on by population growth, climate change, or water and food shortages?

Similar questions might be raised with regard to the problem of the region's economies. A region in which most states have not been able to wean themselves from dependence on rent is not one likely to prosper in a world that gives pride of place to free markets and the cultivation of each state's comparative advantage, whatever their merits. Just what finished products might most Middle Eastern states produce better and more cheaply than other states in the global market? Setting aside such fanciful ideas as building the knowledge-based economies of the future and habituating populations to the free market, how will it be possible to halt the economic free fall that has devastated parts of the region? How will it be possible to ratchet up performance in economies that are now treading water?

Condoleezza Rice's New Middle East got off to a rocky start. Its prospects have not improved with time.

# NOTES

## Preface

1. Peter Catterall, "What (if Anything) Is Distinctive about Contemporary History," *Journal of Contemporary History* 32 (October 1997), 450.
2. William Faulkner, *Requiem for a Nun* (New York: Vintage International, 2011), 73.

## Chapter 1

1. *World Population Prospects 2019* (New York: United Nations Department of Economic and Social Affairs, Population Division, 2020), https://population.un.org/wpp/Download/Standard/Population/.
2. *Democracy Index 2010: Democracy in Retreat* (London: Economist Intelligence Unit, 2010), https://graphics.eiu.com/PDF/Democracy_Index_2010_web.pdf.
3. Nathan J. Brown, *When Victory Is Not an Option: Islamist Movements in Arab Politics* (Ithaca, NY: Cornell University Press, 2012), 1.
4. *Arab Human Development Report 2004: Towards Freedom in the Arab World* (New York: United Nations Development Programme, 2004), http://hdr.undp.org/en/content/arab-human-development-report-2004.
5. "Remarks by President George W. Bush at the Twentieth Anniversary of the National Endowment for Democracy" (Washington, DC: National Endowment for Democracy, 2003),

http://www.ned.org/remarks-by-president-george-w-bush-at-the-20th-anniversary/.

6. Condoleezza Rice, "Remarks at the American University in Cairo" (Washington, DC: US Department of State, 2005), https://2001-2009.state.gov/secretary/rm/2005/48328.htm.

7. Jason Brownlee, *Democracy Prevention: The Politics of the US-Egyptian Alliance* (Cambridge, UK: Cambridge University Press, 2012).

8. "Secretary Rice Holds a News Conference," *Washington Post*, July 22, 2006, http://www.csmonitor.com/1981/1014/101425.html.

9. Richard N. Haass, "The New Middle East," *Foreign Affairs* (November–December 2006), https://www.foreignaffairs.com/articles/middle-east/2006-11-01/new-middle-east.

**Chapter 2**

1. "Statistics Reveal Casualties since Military Coup in Egypt," *Middle East Monitor*, February 5, 2014, https://www.middleeast monitor.com/20140205-statistics-reveal-casualties-since-military-coup-in-egypt/.

2. See James T. Quinlivan, "Coup-Proofing: Its Practice and Consequences in the Middle East," *International Security* 24 (Autumn 1999), 131–65.

3. "GYBO Manifesto 2.0," Gaza Youth Breaks Out, n.d., https://gazaybo.wordpress.com/about/.

**Chapter 3**

1. "Crisis, Fragile and Failed States: Definitions Used by the CSRC," https://www.lse.ac.uk/international-development/Assets/Documents/PDFs/csrc-background-papers/Definition-of-a-Failed-State.pdf.

2. Anne Bernard, "As Syria's Revolution Sputters, a Chaotic Stalemate," *New York Times*, December 27, 2014, https://www.nytimes.com/2014/12/28/world/as-syrias-revolution-sputters-a-chaotic-stalemate.html.

3. "S/RES/1973%20(2011)," UN Security Council, July 27, 2018, https://www.undocs.org/Home/Mobile?FinalSymbol=S%2FRES%2F1973%2520(2011)&Language=E&DeviceType=Desk top&LangRequested=False.

4. "Syria: UN-Arab League Envoy Warns of Limited Options, Dangers of Fragmentation," UN Information Centre in Cairo, December 30, 2012, http://www.unic-eg.org/eng/?p=5140.

5. Malik al-Abdeh, "Rebels, Inc.," *Foreign Policy*, November 21, 2013, http://foreignpolicy.com/2013/11/21/rebels-inc/.

6. "Letter Dated 26 January 2018 from the Panel of Experts on Yemen Mandated by Security Council Resolution 2342 (2017) Addressed to the President of the Security Council," UN Security Council, January 26, 2018, https://www.securitycouncilrep ort.org.

7. Amr Salahi, "The Evacuation of Homs: Humanitarianism or Ethnic Cleansing?" *Middle East Monitor*, March 29, 2014, https://www.middleeastmonitor.com/20140329-the-evacuation-of-homs-humanitarianism-or-ethnic-cleansing/.

8. *Al-Jazeera*, September 6, 2022, https://www.aljazeera.com/news/2022/9/6/syria-seizes-hummus-bowls-made-out-of-captagon.

9. Jeffrey Goldberg, "The Obama Doctrine, *The Atlantic*, April 2016, http://www.theatlantic.com/magazine/archive/2016/04/the-obama-doctrine/471525/.

10. Brian Michael Jenkins, "Terrorism and Beyond: A Twenty-First Century Perspective," *Studies in Conflict and Terrorism* 24 (2001), https://books.google.com/books?id=unFKCAAAQBAJ&pg= PT14&lpg=PT14&dq=Terrorism+and+beyond+%22flaming+ bananas%22&source=bl&ots=PC-raPznQ9&sig=ACfU3U0 TAuTQFodnCaC9ungjpAEaUo1qlw&hl=en&sa=X&ved= 2ahUKEwj27dKFk6_AhUmEEQIHW6UDrcQ6AF6BAgh EAM#v=onepage&q=Terrorism%20and%20beyond%20%22flam ing%20bananas%22&f=false.

11. "Iran: Government Mismanagement Compounds Covid-19 Crisis," *Human Rights Watch*, August 19, 2021, https://www. hrw.org/news/2021/08/19/iran-government-mismanagement-compounds-covid-19-crisis.

Chapter 4

1. "Mideast: The 'Worst Case' Theory," *Washington Post*, February 25, 1978, https://www.washingtonpost.com/archive/politics/1978/02/25/mideast-the-worst-case-theory/0896c3c3-5a4a-422e-bdb0-28adeb2d0d39/.

2. Kelley Beaucar Vlahos, "Remembering Powell's Revealing Exchange with Madeleine Albright," *Responsible Statecraft*, October 18, 2021, https://responsiblestatecraft.org/2021/10/18/remembering-powells-revealing-exchange-with-madeleine-albright/.

3. Ryan Lizza, "Leading from Behind," *New Yorker*, April 26, 2011, https://www.newyorker.com/news/news-desk/leading-from-behind.

4. Benjamin Mueller, "British Leaks Describe Trump's 'Act of Diplomatic Vandalism' on Iran Deal," *New York Times*, July 13, 2019, https://www.nytimes.com/2019/07/13/world/europe/britain-leaks-press-freedom.html.

5. Joseph Biden, "Remarks by President Biden at the GCC + 3 Summit Meeting, July 16, 2022," White House (website), July 16, 2022, https://www.whitehouse.gov/briefing-room/speeches-remarks/2022/07/16/remarks-by-president-biden-at-the-gcc-3-summit-meeting/.

6. *Russian Strategy in the Middle East* (Santa Monica, CA: Rand Corporation, 2017), https//www.rand.org/pubs/perspectives/PE236.html.

7. James Sladden, et al., *Russian Strategy in the Middle East* (Santa Monica, CA: RAND Corporation, 2017), https://www.rand.org/pubs/perspectives/PE236.html; Scott Wilson, "Obama Dismisses Russia as 'Regional Power' Acting out of Weakness," *Washington Post*, March 25, 2014, https://www.washingtonpost.com/world/national-security/obama-dismisses-russia-as-regional-power-acting-out-of-weakness/2014/03/25/1e5a678e-b439-11e3-b899-20667de76985_story.html?utm_term=.a77e90287fe2.

8. *Shared Vision, Common Action: A Stronger Europe, European Union Global Strategy* (n.p.: European Union, June 2016), https://eeas.europa.eu/sites/eeas/files/eugs_review_web_0.pdf.

9. "Iranian President Cites Late Ayatollah as Saying Jewish State 'Must Be Wiped from the Map of the World,'" *CNN Wire*, October 27, 2005, http://www.cnn.com/2005/US/10/26/wednesday/.

10. Kingdom of Saudi Arabia, "Vision 2030," n.d., https://www.saudiembassy.net/vision-2030.

11. Jeffrey Goldberg, "Saudi Crown Prince: Iran's Supreme Leader 'Makes Hitler Look Good,'" *The Atlantic*, April 2, 2018, https://www.theatlantic.com/international/archive/2018/04/mohammed-bin-salman-iran-israel/557036/.

12. Patrick Wintour, "US Backtracks on Iran-Focused Conference in Poland after Objections," *The Guardian*, January 23, 2019, https://www.theguardian.com/world/2019/jan/23/us-backtracks-on-iran-focused-conference-in-poland-after-objections.

Chapter 5

1. *Arab Human Development Report 2009: Challenges to Human Security in the Arab Countries* (New York: United Nations Development Programme, 2009), http://www.arab-hdr.org/Prev iousReports/2009/2009.aspx.

2. Navtej Dhillon and Amina Fahmy, "Urban and Young: The Future of the Middle East" (Washington, DC: Brookings Institution, June 11, 2008), https://www.brookings.edu/opini ons/urban-and-young-the-future-of-the-middle-east/.

3. Lina Eklund et al., "Societal Drought Vulnerability and the Syrian Climate-Conflict Nexus Are Better Explained by Agriculture than Meteorology," *Communications Earth & Environment*, April 6, 2022, https://www.nature.com/articles/s43247-022-00405-w#arti cle-info.

4. Keith Johnson, "U.S. Warns of 'Catastrophic Failure' of Iraq's Mosul Dam," *Foreign Policy*, February 29, 2016, http://foreignpol icy.com/2016/02/29/u-s-warns-of-catastrophic-failure-of-iraqs-mosul-dam/.

5. G. Zittis et al, "Climate Change and Weather Extremes in the Eastern Mediterranean and Middle East," *Reviews of Geophysics*, June 28, 2022, https://agupubs.onlinelibrary.wiley.com/doi/full/10.1029/2021RG000762; Karina Tsui, "The Middle East Is Warming Up Twice as Fast as the Rest of the World," *Washington Post*, September 7, 2022, https://www.washingtonpost.com/world/2022/09/07/middle-east-mediterranean-climate-change/.

6. *Arab Human Development Report 2005: Towards the Rise of Women in the Arab World*, (New York: United Nations Development Programme, 2005), hdr.undp.org/sites/default/files/rbas_ahdr2005_en.pdf.

7. *The World's Muslims: Religion, Politics, and Society* (Washington, DC: Pew Research Center's Forum on Religion & Public Life, 2013), http://www.pewforum.org/2013/04/30/the-worlds-musl ims-religion-politics-society-women-in-society/.

8. "Kuwait Voluntary National Review 2019," https://sustainable development.un.org/content/documents/23384Kuwait_VNR_FI NAL.PDF.

9. *Arab Human Development Report 2003: Building a Knowledge Society* (New York: United Nations Development Programme, 2003), hdr. undp.org/sites/default/files/rbas_ahdr2003_en.pdf.

10. United Nations Department of Economic and Social Affairs, *The Millennial Development Goals Report: Facing Challenges and Looking beyond 2015* (New York, 2016), file:///C:/Users/James%20 Gelvin/Dropbox/My%20PC%20(DESKTOP-PFTMJ4E)/ Downloads/E_ESCWA_EDGD_2013_1-EN.pdf.

# FURTHER READING

**General Works on the Middle East**
Beinin, Joel. *Workers and Peasants in the Modern Middle East*. Cambridge,
    UK: Cambridge University Press, 2001.
Gelvin, James L. *The Modern Middle East: A History*. 5th ed.
    New York: Oxford University Press, 2020.
Sadiki, Larbi, ed. *Routledge Handbook of Middle East Politics*.
    London: Routledge, 2020.

**Topical Books**
Bayat, Asef. *Revolutionary Life: The Everyday of the Arab Spring*.
    Cambridge, MA: Harvard University Press, 2021.
Beinin, Joel. *Workers and Thieves: Labor Movements and Popular Uprisings
    in Tunisia and Egypt*. Stanford, CA: Stanford University Press, 2015.
Cammett, Melani, and Ishac Diwan, eds. *The Political Economy of the
    Arab Uprisings*. London: Routledge, 2019.
Di Giovanni, Janine. *In the Morning They Came for Us: Dispatches from
    Syria*. New York: Liveright, 2016.
Einhorn, Robert. "Debating the Iran Nuclear Deal." Washington,
    DC: Brookings Institution, August 12, 2105. https://www.brooki
    ngs.edu/series/debating-the-iran-deal/ (last accessed April
    19, 2016).
Gelvin, James L. *The Arab Uprisings: What Everyone Needs to Know*. 2nd
    ed. New York: Oxford University Press, 2015.
Gelvin, James L., ed. *The Contemporary Middle East in an Age of Upheaval*.
    Stanford, CA: Stanford University Press, 2020.

Gerges, Fawaz. *ISIS: A History*. Princeton, NJ: Princeton University Press, 2016.

Goldberg, Jeffrey. "The Obama Doctrine." *Atlantic*, April 2016. http://www.theatlantic.com/magazine/archive/2016/04/the-obama-doctrine/471525.

Haas, Mark L., and David W. Lesch, eds. *The Arab Spring: The Hope and Reality of the Uprisings*. 2nd ed. Boulder, CO: Westview, 2016.

Hanssen, Jens, and Max Weiss, eds. *Arabic Thought against the Authoritarian Age: Towards an Intellectual History of the Present*. Cambridge, UK: Cambridge University Press, 2018.

Lynch, Marc. *The New Arab Wars: Uprisings and Anarchy in the Middle East*. New York: Public Affairs, 2016.

Matthiesen, Toby. *Sectarian Gulf: Bahrain, Saudi Arabia, and the Arab Spring That Wasn't*. Stanford, CA: Stanford University Press, 2013.

Mazur, Kevin. *Revolution in Syria*. Cambridge, UK: Cambridge University Press, 2021.

Owen, Roger. *The Rise and Fall of Arab Presidents for Life*. Cambridge, MA: Harvard University Press, 2012.

Phillips, Christopher. The *Battle for Syria: International Rivalry in the New Middle East*. New Haven, CT: Yale University Press, 2016.

"The Politics of Sectarianism." POMEPS Studies 4. Washington, DC: Project on Middle East Political Science, November 13, 2013. https://pomeps.org/2013/11/14/the-politics-of-sectarianism/.

Ward, Christopher, and Sandra Ruckstuhl. *Water Scarcity, Climate Change and Conflict in the Middle East: Securing Livelihoods, Building Peace*. London: I. B. Tauris, 2017.

Worth, Robert H. *A Rage for Order: The Middle East in Turmoil, from Tahrir Square to ISIS*. New York: Farrar, Straus, and Giroux, 2016.

**Websites**

The Conversation (wide-ranging content from academics and researchers). https://theconversation.com/us.

Foreign Policy. www.foreignpolicy.com.

International Crisis Group. www.crisisgroup.org.

Jadaliyya (Ezine of the Arab Studies Institute). www.jadaliyya.com.

al-Jazeera (English version of popular Arab newspaper based in Qatar). http://english.aljazeera.net.

Middle East Research and Information Project (MERIP). http://www.merip.org.

al-Monitor (reports by journalists based in the Middle East). http://al-monitor.com/pulse/home.html.

Project on Middle East Political Science (POMEPS). https://pomeps.org/.

Wikileaks. https://wikileaks.org/.

# INDEX

For the benefit of digital users, indexed terms that span two pages (e.g., 52–53) may, on occasion, appear on only one of those pages.

Figures are indicated by f following the page number